The Men Who Made

MOTHERWELL FOOTBALL CLUB 1946-2001

The Men Who Made

Motherwell Football Club 1946-2001

Jim Jeffrey and Genge Fry

First published in 2001 by Tempus Publishing

Reprinted in 2009 by
The History Press
The Mill, Brimscombe Port
Stroud, Gloucestershire, GL5 2QG
www.thehistorypress.co.uk

British Library Cataloguing in Publication Data.
A catalogue record for this book is available from the British Library.

ISBN 978 0 7524 2191 9

Typesetting and origination by Tempus Publishing
Printed in Great Britain

FOREWORD
by John Swinburne

I first came into contact with Jim Jeffrey and Genge Fry back in the late 1980s. At that time I was producing the Motherwell Football Club matchday programme. This was a one-man project and in addition to my everyday job as commercial manager at the club.

As fans will no doubt agree, there are few things worse than having the views of one individual presented to them in their match programme and therefore I was extremely grateful when both Jim and Genge agreed to help out with copy. Genge is a life-long Motherwell fan and he has the best collection of old programmes and other memorablia that I have ever known. He immediately put these at our disposal and this enhanced our programme enormously.

The arrangement worked out so well that within a few years Jim was actually producing the programme on behalf of Motherwell Football Club and my involvement became less and less until, due to other commitments, I virtually opted out. Jim took over with Genge as his main support.

One of the earlier projects which Jim and I decided to embark upon was an A to Z of Motherwell FC and we ran this for a couple of seasons in the programme. This helped spark off the idea of Jim producing a book which would cover every player ever to have played in a League fixture for Motherwell since the Second World War.

I had the pleasure of reading through a draft copy of their book and while our opinions of some players may differ, this is part of the magical lure of football and their compilation is very accurate. The beauty, and indeed purpose, of the book is to bring back a host of memories for young and old alike.

I am sure Motherwell supporters will love recalling the careers of the many great players to have represented the club over the years. I can highly recommend this book by Jim and Genge to all Motherwell fans. I only hope that at some time in the future they will produce a publication which covers all of the club's results. This would then complement this book perfectly.

Motherwell FC Scottish FA Cup winners, 1951/52. From left to right, back row: Kilmarnock (captain), Cox, Paton, Johnston, Redpath, Shaw. Front row: Sloan, Humphries, Kelly, Watson, Aitkenhead.

Acknowledgements

This book would have been impossible to compile without the help of a number of people. In covering the careers of the many Motherwell players to have represented the club since the end of the last war, we were conscious that their stories would be incomplete if we did not include their exploits at other clubs. We are therefore very grateful to the programme editors and historians of many other clubs. Special thanks are due to: Duncan Carmichael (Ayr United), Peter Rundo (Dundee United), Alistair Blair (St Johnstone), Brian Johnson (Hibernian), Pat Woods (Celtic), Robert McElroy (Rangers), Allan Grieve (Stirling Albion), John Litster (Raith Rovers), Richard Cairns and John Livingston (Kilmarnock) and Alastair MacLachlan (St Mirren).

It is to Alastair that we owe the largest debt, as he patiently trawled through much of the club's history when working on the Motherwell match programme and then graciously handed over his research when he was 'transferred' to St Mirren. Alastair also interviewed many of the club's former players and these interviews, together with those carried out subsequently, were a valuable source of information.

David Thomson of the Scottish Football League made his office's club records available on several occasions and for that we are extremely grateful. Similarly, David Walker at the *Sunday Post* was also extremely helpful and allowed us access to back copies of his newspaper.

George Brown and the late Freddie Pollok of East Kilbride were also an enormous help; indeed, this book owes much to a very pleasant evening spent in Freddie's house several years ago chatting about Motherwell. Little did we imagine that from that night this project would grow and we owe both men a great 'thank you'.

Finally, a book such as this relied on the many anecdotes and records which Motherwell supporters deliberately or unwittingly put our way. In this respect Terry Willoughby and John Swinburne were of enormous help. John, of course, produced the club's *Centenary History* in 1986, documented the club's Scottish Cup triumph of 1991, and latterly published a collection of the club's photographs. He is a walking encyclopaedia on the club and his enthusiasm for all things 'Motherwell' shines through; we were delighted when he agreed to produce a foreword for this book.

Introduction

It was compiling the Motherwell match programme which first sowed the seeds of this book in our minds. The programme would not only look forward to the match that day but inevitably put the match in the context of the club's history. Great names from the past would crop up and it was frustrating that there was no single publication that covered the careers of these players.

Countless hours spent trawling through old newspapers at the Mitchell Library and the local library in Motherwell convinced us that the material to compile a 'Who's Who' of Motherwell was there, but widely scattered. When other clubs brought out similar volumes to the one we intended it was clear the task could be completed. Little did we know just how long it would take!

The statistical information in this book is possibly the key to judging the impact of a player, but before the 1970s records were sketchy and unreliable. Contemporary newspapers were a great source of information but occasionally contradictory. Motherwell lovingly produced club handbooks and these were a wonderful source of information, as were club programmes – both those produced by Motherwell and their opponents. Where conflicts between the press and the official publications have arisen we have taken the club information to be the more accurate.

We decided at an early stage to concentrate solely, as many other club histories have, on League appearances as a criteria for inclusion. This was due to the fact that the various cup competitions in which Motherwell played have occasionally thrown up 'meaningless' matches, particularly at the end of League Cup sections or in 'second leg' matches where the first leg was convincingly won. The acid test of any player's worth seems to have been inclusion in League matches. Furthermore, to have included cup matches would have left us with a dilemma of where to 'draw the line' as the temptation would have been to go beyond Scottish and League Cup ties and then include European, Summer Cup, Texaco Cup, Anglo Scottish Cup and Lanarkshire Cup matches and so forth.

Finally we had to conclude at some point. We chose the end of the 1999/2000 season. The players listed in this book therefore are those who played in League matches in the post-war era up to the start of the 2000/01 season. However, the sands of time continue to shift and some players or ex-players were already on the move as this book went to press. A book such as this is never truly complete, and is by necessity somewhat abridged.

If anyone has any further information they can add to the profiles of the players contained herein, it would be most gratefully received.

The Scottish team being introduced to HRH Duke of Gloucester. Willie Redpath starred for Scotland in this match against England on 4 April 1951. Scotland won the match 3-2.

A

Derek ADAMS

A centre forward, Derek was signed from Ross County in 1998 for a fee believed to be in the region of £175,000. He had been a prolific scorer with the Dingwall club and was soon amongst the goals for Motherwell, grabbing his first against Celtic. However, he could not keep a regular place and in October of the 1999/2000 season he was loaned out to First Division Ayr United, only to return to Motherwell in a midfield role as the season ended. Prior to serving Ross County, Derek had played briefly with Aberdeen and Burnley.

Appearances 43 Goals 4

Derek Adams

Charlie Aitken

Charlie AITKEN

A wing-half noted for his heading and tackling, Charlie joined Motherwell in 1949 from Arniston Rangers and proved a steady and reliable performer. An impeccable sportsman, he became a stalwart in the side; so much so that in both 1957 and 1958 he won the Player of the Year award. In 1966 he added the prestigious Scottish Players' Union Award for services to football. He played for the Scotland 'B' side against England 'B' at Birmingham in 1957 and one year later served the Scottish League against both the League of Ireland and Irish League. Aitken, who was born in Gorebridge, won few domestic honours, although he did play in the 1954 side which lost the League Cup final to Hearts. Perhaps the highlight for Charlie was playing in the 1965 Summer Cup final victory over Dundee United.

Signed by George Stevenson as

Johnny Aitkenhead

a seventeen-year-old, Charlie made a scoring first team debut against Celtic in April 1951, in a match which Motherwell lost 1-3. In his next game, against Raith, he scored again as the club recorded a 3-2 win. He was then lost to National Service, but after being demobbed in 1954 he came back in dramatic fashion, netting a last minute equaliser in a Scottish Cup semi-final tie against Celtic which ended 2-2. However, that was his only appearance of the 1953/54 season . Nevertheless, with his National Service behind him he was able to stake a regular claim to first team football.

His final competitive match came on 12 February 1966 against St Johnstone. After seventeen years of loyal service he was awarded a testimonial and, in an emotional match on 24 May 1967, Motherwell drew 1-1 with Rangers. Undoubtedly Charlie was one of the all-time greats at Fir Park.

Appearances 313 Goals 36

Johnny AITKENHEAD

Nicknamed 'The Daddler', Johnny was a tricky outside-left who gave the club distinguished service for almost a decade. Signed from Hibernian, he had started his career with Queen's Park and could well have been a Hibernian legend had his spell at Easter Road not coincided with the forward line known collectively as 'The Famous Five'. Aitkenhead did make his mark with Hibs, but it would be his 1949 transfer to Motherwell after recovering from a serious leg injury that made his career.

He made his Motherwell bow in a League match on New Year's Day 1949 and scored twice in the 3-1 win at Albion Rovers. For the following five seasons he was very much a regular and capable of contributing quite a few goals, despite his wide berth.

League Cup goals were a speciality of his, and it was fitting that he played in the side which beat Hibernian in the 1950 League Cup final at Hampden Park. Indeed, en route to Hampden he had notched up two goals in the pulsating 4-3 semi-final win against Ayr United. He missed out on a remarkable double that season as the club lost 0-1 to Celtic in the Scottish Cup final. However, he made up for the disappointment by playing in the 1952 team which won Motherwell's first ever Scottish Cup.

Capped 3 times by the Scottish League, Johnny was a penalty expert and enjoyed a spell in which he netted 40 consecutive penalties. He ended his senior career

with a brief spell at neighbouring Hamilton Academical.
Appearances 171 Goals 49

Jack AITKENHEAD
With Andy Paton dominating the centre half role in the post-war Motherwell side, Jack Aitkenhead became a long-term understudy. Reliable when called upon, he was never able to oust Paton from the first team and in an astonishing nine year stint made just 7 League appearances. Signed in 1948 from Stoneyburn United, he stayed until released in the summer of 1957.
Appearances 7 Goals 0

Ian ALEXANDER
A native of Glasgow, Ian went from Leicester Juveniles to Rotherham United and then in 1983 moved to Motherwell. Signed by Jock Wallace, he played at right-back and was an impressively fit defender, but he was unable to settle at Fir Park. He moved to Morton in 1984 and then on to Pezoporikos Larnaca of Cyprus before returning to England to play with Bristol Rovers.
Appearances 24 Goals 2

John ANDERSON
Anderson came to Fir Park in 1949 from Newarthill Hearts along with Jim Forrest. As an inside forward, he had scored 50 goals for Newarthill the previous season, and went on to score 12 for Motherwell reserves in 1949/50. He also played his only game for the first team that term on 29 October, away to Queen of the South. Sadly, he was released at the end of the season.
Appearances 1 Goals 0

Tom ANDERSON
Tom was one of those post-war players at Fir Park who stayed with the club for many years, only to make a single appearance. In Tom's case his one outing was against Rangers on the final day of the 1947/48 season, helping Motherwell to a 1-1 draw. He was signed in 1943 from SS&E Athletic and was granted a free transfer in 1949. He won a Scottish Cup winners medal with Clyde in 1955.
Appearances 1 Goals 0

Ian ANGUS
One of the legendary Bobby Calder's finds for Aberdeen, Ian went straight from the highly-rated Eastercraigs BC to the Dons in 1976. By 1980 he was in the first team and in 1985 won a League championship medal. He was on the bench when Aberdeen captured the European Cup Winners Cup. In 1986 he moved to Dundee as part of a deal that

Ian Angus

Dougie Arnott

saw Robert Connor move to Pittodrie. He was a regular in the Dundee side until Tommy McLean signed him for Motherwell in 1990. One year later both were celebrating Motherwell's Scottish Cup win, with Angus scoring a goal in the final itself.

His classy approach to the game was immediately obvious and, in a team that boasted talents such as Davie Cooper and Stevie Kirk, he was an ideal foil. A good worker, he gave the side a midfield balance and in four seasons was reliable and well-liked. He moved to Clyde in August 1994 when he was in his early thirties and beginning to lose pace.
Appearances 70/17 Goals 8

Dougie ARNOTT
If there was an award for popularity, Dougie Arnott would be a contender. A marvellous little striker, his sheer enthusiasm and determination won him many admirers, but arguably it was his wonderful goalscoring record against the Old Firm that endeared him most to the Motherwell supporters.

He was a late starter by modern standards, playing junior football with Lesmahagow and Pollok before Tommy McLean recruited him to the Motherwell cause in October 1986. In his first few seasons he contributed very few goals, but gradually became a regular marksman.

Picking the best goals in Dougie's career is no easy task. He scored two against Celtic in the 1991 Scottish Cup semi-final. A few weeks later he had another brace, this time in a 3-0 home win over Rangers, when the Ibrox side needed a win to take the title.

Dougie bowed out in the 1998/99 season and scored his last goal in a memorable 6-2 victory over Hibernian at Fir Park. Throughout his Motherwell career he had been a busy forward, and the enduring image is of a small, terrier-like striker, snapping at the heels of some of the finest Scottish defenders – to good effect!
Appearances 240 Goals 59

B

Hervé BACQUE
This twenty-two-year-old French midfielder flitted briefly into the Fir Park picture in the 1998/99 season. A native of Bordeaux, he had played with Lorient and Monaco in France before enjoying a brief spell with Luton Town in England. Although clever on the ball, he could not establish himself at Fir Park and played

in just one match, as a substitute; a 0-1 defeat at Dundee in February 1999.
Appearances 0/1 Goals 0

Craig BAILLIE
Ordinarily, a ratio of 1 goal every 2 games would ensure a player a high profile at a club. Alas, for Craig this was not the case. Talented and tricky as he was, Craig was not seen as a long-term prospect and left the club just months after joining from Brighton. He made his debut in April 1964 and scored in a 2-0 win over Kilmarnock.

Born in Airdrie, he had originally joined the south coast club from Kirkintilloch Rob Roy. Later in his career he played for Distillery in Belfast.
Appearances 6 Goals 3

Alex BAIN
In the list of prolific centre forwards to have served Motherwell, there should surely be space left for Alex Bain. He came to the club as a junior and was soon a prolific marksman in the reserves. He transferred his marksmanship to the first team and was performing well when Bill Shankly signed him for Huddersfield Town. He scored frequently for Huddersfield too, but did not settle, and later played with Chesterfield, Falkirk and Bournemouth.

Bain joined Motherwell in 1954 from Cockenzie Star and was a native of Edinburgh. Doubtless he would have enjoyed representing Motherwell against Hearts in the League Cup final in 1954. A printer by trade, his biggest asset was probably his heading ability, which belied his lack of inches. In moving to Huddersfield he was following the same path as another great Motherwell forward, Jimmy Watson.
Appearances 23 Goals 10

Gerry BAKER
Like his brother Joe, Gerald Austin Baker is remembered as an exciting centre forward. Throughout his seven club career he was always a prolific marksman and a delight to watch. Baker's, and perhaps Fir Park's, misfortune was that he arrived on the scene at the same time as St John, Quinn, Weir and Hunter. In short, there was no guarantee of first team football.

Gerry was born in 1938 in New York, served Larkhall Thistle and then moved to London. Motherwell signed him from Ted Drake's Chelsea for £750 in November 1957. Almost instantly the nineteen-year-old won a Second Eleven Cup medal and he made his first team bow against Dundee in April of that year. It is a little surprising that he managed only 10 League outings before moving to St Mirren in 1958.

He cost the Paisley side £2,000 in November of that year and scored

Alex Bain

the winning goal on his debut against Hibernian, made all the more sweet by the fact that his more illustrious brother was in the Hibs line-up. Gerry was an instant hit in Paisley and as the season continued he scored 13 goals in 12 games as St Mirren pulled clear of relegation worries. Moreover, he completed the season with a Scottish Cup winner's medal, netting in every round of the 1959 tourney. He proved a thorn in the flesh to Motherwell as the years rolled by, netting no fewer than 5 times against Motherwell in little over 2 seasons.

More spectacularly, he scored 10 goals in St Mirren's record 15-0 win over Glasgow University in the Scottish Cup first round on 30 January 1960 (his brother was to hit 9 for Hibs against Peebles, in a remarkable family double). In 1960 he was sold to Manchester City for £17,000, but he rarely showed the same form and was sold on to Hibs in 1962. Ironically, one of his first matches took him to Love Street to face his former team-mates and, although warmly greeted, he left to a chorus of boos having netted the winner in a 3-2 win. He was Hibs' top scorer in 1962/63, but left in December 1963 to join Ipswich Town. For four years he served the Suffolk side and in 135 League games he scored a creditable 58 goals. This convinced Coventry City to sign him in November 1967 but his stay was to be short. He had only 27 games before he was off to Brentford in 1969, where he scored 2 goals in only 8 games. For a short period he managed Racing Club Warwick and Nuneaton in English non-League football.

Crawford Baptie

Gerry had one international cap, for the USA, and was undoubtedly a finisher who would have been a superb replacement for Ian St John. However, he was unwilling to hang around and wait for his chance, and he must go down as a clear case of 'one that got away'.

Appearances 10 Goals 3

Paul BAKER

A powerful big English striker, he was signed by Tommy McLean from Hartlepool United in 1992. He scored only once in 9 games and was moved on to Gillingham, having failed to convince the Fir Park faithful that he was the striker of their dreams.

Appearances 9 Goals 1

Crawford BAPTIE

One of Scotland's more popular players, Crawford came to Lanarkshire from Falkirk in January 1986, in a deal that took Rab Stewart to Brockville. Capable of playing at either centre half or up front, he played 33 League games for Motherwell before Tommy McLean moved him back to Falkirk. Crawford

stated that it was his reluctance to give up his job in the motor trade and go full-time which infuriated Tommy McLean and led to his swift return to Brockville. Big and strong, he later served Hamilton Accies. In 1999 Crawford was persuaded to return to Falkirk as general manager.
Appearances 20/13 Goals 3

Willie BARCLAY
Barclay was with Larkhall Thistle when Motherwell offered him terms in 1945, and he stayed for four years before moving to Bury in 1949 for a useful £4,000. A flying winger, he was tricky and creative and his debut was memorable, coming in a 3-0 win at Rangers on the opening day of the 1946/47 season. A tally of 6 goals from 54 outings seems scant reward for an above average player.
Appearances 54 Goals 6

Willie Barclay

Jim BEATON
Jim played just four games for Motherwell following his 1967 signing from Carluke Rovers. An outside-right, he faced stiff competition for a first team jersey and was released twelve months after joining.
Appearances 4 Goals 0

Ray Blair

Kenny BLACK
Probably best known for his stints at Rangers, Hearts and Airdrie. A mere 17 games for Motherwell reveal that Kenny never really fitted into the Fir Park scene. He was signed in 1983 as part of a player swap with Rangers and sold to Hearts in June 1984 for £60,000. Kenny played in England with Portsmouth but really stood out at Airdrie. He was an integral part of the Diamonds team that became renowned for its cup-fighting traditions.
Appearances 17 Goals 0

Ian BLAIR
Playing twice in the 1963/64 season, in the immediate aftermath of Bobby

Tom Boyd

Roberts' transfer to England, his first game was a 1-3 home defeat to St Johnstone. A week later he was in the side that was held to a goal-less draw at Partick Thistle. He was freed at the end of the campaign along with Bobby Russell, Jim Lonie, Jim Seith, and Willie McSeveney.

Appearances 2 Goals 0

Ray BLAIR

Ray Blair was a former St Johnstone midfielder who came to Motherwell in 1984. He played over 50 games, scoring 8 times, before moving to East Fife as a makeweight in the deal to bring Stevie Kirk to Motherwell. Blair, who was fairly small and compact, could also count Dumbarton amongst his football-related employers. A determined character, he had more skill than he was given credit for.

Appearances 38/14 Goals 8

John BOYD

A left-back, John was signed from Clydebank in 1968 on a free transfer. However, he was unable to make a mark at Fir Park and left on a free transfer to Clyde within months of arriving. His only game for the club came at Fir Park in March 1968, when Motherwell drew with Falkirk 1-1.

Appearances 1 Goals 0

Jim BOYD

A £20,000 purchase from Clyde in 1978, Jim was another defender who could not quite establish himself at Motherwell. He played 11 games, 2 of them as a sub, before returning to Clyde the following year. A popular player with the Bully Wee, he never had the same impact at Fir Park.

Appearances 9/2 Goals 0

Tom BOYD

Perhaps one of the finest full-backs to serve the club since the legendary Ben Ellis in the 1930s, Boyd was speedy, direct and quick-tackling. He was the classic overlapping full-back who could play equally well in midfield.

He joined the club in 1983 as a YTS signing and made rapid progress until he became one of the youngest club captains in the Premier Division. Much of his early progress was due to Frank Connor, who drove Tom on to win five Under-18 caps for Scotland. His incisive play and shrewd thinking won him many admirers and he made his 'B' international debut for Scotland at Fir Park against Yugoslavia in March 1990; by which time he already had five Under-21 caps. That launched him on a national career, which eventually brought him membership of the SFA's

Hall of Fame, reserved for those with over 50 national caps. He made his international debut as a sub at Hampden Park against Romania in September 1990, during a European Championship tie, and started a Scotland match for the first time a few weeks later against Switzerland.

However, impressive as he was on the international stage, it was at Fir Park that he made his reputation, linking superbly with Davie Cooper, and it was fitting that he should bow out of Lanarkshire holding the 1991 Scottish Cup aloft.

He joined Chelsea for a fee of £800,000 shortly after the final but failed to settle in London and returned to Scotland with Celtic, in a swap deal which took Tony Cascarino to Stamford Bridge. Ironically, on one of Boyd's first returns to Fir Park with Celtic he conceded a penalty and was sent off for fouling Dougie Arnott!

Appearances 256 Goals 6

Ged BRANNAN

This strong midfielder joined Motherwell during Pat Nevin's reign as chief executive. Nevin, having been a Tranmere star himself, was adept at using his Prenton Park connection in his time at Fir Park, and Brannan was a fine acquisition. A combative midfielder, he could number skilful passing and great dead-ball accuracy amongst his list of talents. He was actually signed from Manchester City, where he had endured a wretched time following a big money move from Tranmere.

Brannan scored several memorable goals for Motherwell, including a couple against Celtic and Hearts. However, Ged infuriated Motherwell supporters when, just hours after a shock Scottish Cup exit to Ayr United, he announced that he was going to play international football for the Caymen Islands and thereby miss a crucial game with Hearts.

Appearances 58 Goals 10

Gordon BREMNER

A cultured inside forward, Gordon joined Motherwell in January 1946 from Arsenal for £2,750 and stayed for five years before being given a free transfer. Those who saw him described him as an elegant player with excellent passing ability. His older brother, Hutton Bremner, also played for Motherwell. Gordon won a wartime cap against England in the 1942/43 season.

Appearances 98 Goals 16

Donald BRIMS

A tall player, Donald joined Motherwell in 1957 from Arniston Thistle and went on to play in 11 matches at wing-half or inside forward. He moved on a free transfer in 1958. Five of his games came

Ged Brannan

Gordon Bremner

in the 1956/57 season and Motherwell lost them all.
Appearances 11 Goals 0

Billy BROWN
Recruited from Hull City in 1970, Billy was a stocky half-back who had a short run at the beginning of the 1971/72 season. His last game for Motherwell proved quite memorable, coming as it did in an astonishing 3-8 defeat at Partick Thistle in December 1971. It mattered little that Billy scored in that debacle. He moved to Raith Rovers on a free transfer in 1973 and helped them win the Second Division title. Cruciate ligament damage forced him to retire from the game at the tender age of twenty-seven. Thereafter he coached Raith Rovers reserves, Newtongrange Star and Musselburgh Athletic, before teaming up with Jim Jeffries at Berwick, Falkirk and Hearts. Although he helped steer Hearts to the Scottish Cup in 1998, he was sacked by the Edinburgh club in 2000, but he soon followed Jefferies to Bradford City.
Appearances 9 Goals 0

James BROWN
Brown played in just one game for Motherwell, during the 1957/58 season. He filled the number two jersey in a 0-3 defeat at Dundee before being released at the end of the season. Prior to playing with Motherwell he had been with Bathgate.
Appearances 1 Goals 0

John BROWN
Centre forward in the 1946/47 season, John (known as 'Buster') remarkably scored 16 goals in only 19 games. He started the season in blistering form, hitting both goals in the 2-4 defeat against Rangers (thereby netting the first official Motherwell goals in the post-war era), a single in the 1-3 defeat from Morton and then a hat-trick in the 6-1 demolition of Queen of the South. He scored six goals in the League Cup and another two in the Scottish Cup as the club battled through to a memorable semi-final clash with Hibernian that lasted 142 minutes. John had signed for Motherwell after the trial match in August 1943 from Kello Rovers.
Appearances 19 Goals 16

Robert BROWN
Signed from Polkemmet Juniors in 1951, Robert was unfortunate to be at Fir Park when Cox, Paton and Redpath had tied up the half-back positions. He manfully

stuck to his task and provided excellent cover but his 5 appearances were scant reward for his ability. He was freed in 1956 and joined Workington Town in Cumbria.
Appearances 5 Goals 0

Stuart BROWN
In 1955 Stuart was snapped up by Motherwell from Beith. A clever and creative player, he was transformed from a striker into a full-back. He stayed for five years until he realised that displacing players such as Kilmarnock, McSeveney and Shaw was not very likely. He moved in 1959, having played two dozen games in the League.
Appearances 24 Goals 0

Stevie BRYCE
A red-headed striker, Bryce officially joined Motherwell in June 1987 from Motherwell BC. For six years he threatened to break into the side, and played well in reserve matches. However, his 21 League games failed to produce a single goal and in February of 1993 he moved to Ayr United.
Appearances 6/15 Goals 0

John BRYDEN
Yet another victim of the Kilmarnock-Shaw full-back monopoly, Bryden was unable to command a regular place. The young left-back, having managed only 4 games, moved on. Originally signed in 1952 from Motherwell Juniors, he received a free transfer in the summer of 1955.
Appearances 4 Goals 0

Ramsay BRYSON
A clever outside-right who never made the impression expected at Fir Park, Bryson was signed in 1968 from Dalziel High School. He was to be freed in 1970, having managed a mere 6 League games. He did, however, have the pleasure of scoring a first team goal for the club, in his debut in a 4-0 win away to East Stirlingshire.
Appearances 6 Goals 1

Stevie Bryce

George BURLEY
George had enjoyed a highly successful career with Bobby Robson's Ipswich Town and Scotland before he came to Motherwell in 1989 from Gillingham.

A cultured and energetic right-back, he made over 500 appearances for Ipswich after joining them in 1971. He won 11 Scotland caps and an FA Cup medal before winding down his English career, firstly at Sunderland and then Gillingham. Had it not been for a knee injury sustained in the 1980/81 season, he would have added a UEFA Cup medal to his collection. Given that he more than

George Burley

managed in a side containing players such as Muhren, Thijsen, Butcher, Wark and Mills, it is clear he was one of the best players of his era.

He joined Motherwell as a player initially, but was soon helping out in coaching duties. He stayed until January 1991, before departing for Ayr United, where he learnt the managerial trade. There was a brief return to Motherwell as a player/coach in January 1994 before he accepted the post of Colchester manager. From there he moved back to his beloved Ipswich Town, to manage the Suffolk club that had given him his big break as a player.

At the end of the 1999/2000 season he led Ipswich Town back to the FA Premiership after several desperately near misses. Revered by the Suffolk club as a player, he has inspired similar affection as a manager.

Appearances 57/2 Goals 0

Alex BURNS

Signed from Shotts Bon Accord in August 1991, 'Toastie' was a prolific reserve marksman who netted against Celtic on his full League debut at the start of the 1993/94 season. He was given many openings by manager Tommy McLean, but lacked the consistent goal haul demanded of him. His total of 8 goals in 76 matches preceded his departure to Dutch football with Den Bosch, the precursor to a move to Southend. By 1999 he was back in Scottish Football, playing First Division football, firstly with Raith Rovers and then Livingston.

Appearances 76 Goals 8

Alex Burns

James 'Junior' BURNS
A 1982 signing from Motherwell Boys' Club, this tricky winger joined the club at a bad time. He was only able to play 9 games before being freed in a period of transition. Nevertheless, he had one quite outstanding memory to look back on. In October 1983 he scored as Motherwell defeated Rangers 2-1 at Ibrox. Interestingly, he had played for Scotland Under-18s against their Northern Irish counterparts in 1982/83. He was released in 1984.
Appearances 4/5 Goals 0

Tommy BURNS
Signed for Motherwell from St Mungo's Secondary in 1970 after a shut-out in the Scottish Schools final, Burns proved a more than capable deputy for the injured Keith MacRae when thrown into a Scottish Cup tie against Ayr United. However, he was only able to make 2 outings that term in the League as Motherwell had Fallon, Ritchie and MacRae on their books during that season. He was released at the end of the 1973/74 season. Seldom had an excellent start faded so rapidly.
Appearances 2 Goals 0

C

Benny CAIRNEY
Cairney started with the Lanarkshire junior side Thornliewood United as a centre before getting his big chance with Leicester City. He never settled at Filbert Street and returned home for a month's trial with Celtic. From there he went to Fir Park for a two month trial, before being signed by Bobby Howitt in 1965. By the end of his first season he had won a regular place in the Motherwell side, usually wearing the number 10 shirt. Strongly built and with good pace, he was a useful foil for 'Dixie' Deans up front. In his three seasons at Fir Park he made 39 League appearances, and 4 as a substitute.
Appearances 39/4 Goals 7

John CAMERON
Signed from Gourock Juniors in 1955, John was a left-half who found first team openings restricted. He was freed in 1956, having made it into a mere 6 starting line-ups.
Appearances 6 Goals 0

Benny Cairney

Billy Campbell

Billy CAMPBELL

An Irish international at schoolboy, youth, amateur and full level, this tricky little winger was a Dundee player when Motherwell swooped in July 1968 for his signature, swapping Jim Wilson in the process. He was to play for the Fir Park club for six years and made over 70 first team outings. He was a creator of chances rather than a goalscorer. Released from his contract in 1974, Billy returned to his native Northern Ireland, and Glenavon. Billy had begun his career with Belfast club Distillery and the lure of a return was clear. However, he returned to Fir Park in 1977 as assistant manager under Willie McLean's management.

Appearances 71/5 Goals 6

Bobby CAMPBELL

Left-half Bobby Campbell earned a permanent place in the Motherwell story when he bagged all five goals in a 5-0 win over St Mirren at Love Street in September 1966. Signed by Bobby Howitt in 1965 from the manager's previous club, Morton, he had gained a BSc from Glasgow University and was extremely articulate concerning the game. Bobby was very versatile – he had an extended run at right-back in 1969/70, but his best moments came when fielded further forward. In the 1966/67 season he scored no fewer than 18 First Division goals, thereby becoming the club's top scorer for the campaign, and although he never scaled those heights again he was always likely to contribute something. He was ever-present in the side's Second Division title-winning season of 1968/69, notching 6 goals.

Appearances 157 Goals 36

John CAMPBELL

It was from Kirkintilloch Rob Roy that

Bobby Campbell

Motherwell signed John in 1955. A full-back, he struggled to hold down a first team place and left on a free transfer to Chesterfield in August 1959 having played in only 3 games.
Appearances 3 Goals 0

Neil CANDLISH
Much was expected of Neil, who had all the attributes demanded of a centre forward. He didn't quite fulfil expectations but proved a big hit in Northern Ireland where he joined Glentoran, then Ballymena United and Portadown. Like several other Scottish players at the time, he would train in Scotland during the week and commute to Northern Ireland on Saturdays. Neil had joined Motherwell in 1985, although Tommy McLean initially farmed him out to Wishaw Juniors
Appearances 8/3 Goals 1

Neil Candlish

Jim CAPALDI
Jim arrived at Fir Park from Aston Villa in time for the 1978/79 season, which was unfortunate as the season was to end in relegation. He made his debut, almost inevitably that season, in a defeat. Unfortunately he was unable to find his feet the following season, despite the club being in the First Division.
Appearances 3/8 Goals 0

Bobby CARBERRY
Arriving at Fir Park in the same disastrous relegation season as Jim Capaldi, Bobby fared slightly better. He made his debut the week after the club had lost sensationally 0-8 at Aberdeen – a club record defeat. He featured heavily at the start of the disappointing First Division season that followed and scored his only goal against Hearts. Bobby had cost £25,000 from Alloa in 1979.
Appearances 24/2 Goals 1

Walter CARLYLE
A winger, Carlyle joined Dundee United from Shettleston Juniors in 1960 and stayed at Tannadice for three years. He then came to Motherwell in a £7,000 deal, which seemed a bargain given that he had netted 28 goals for the Tangerines in just 78 matches. Alas, he could not reproduce his United form in the claret and amber of Motherwell and he moved to St Johnstone after just one season as a Steelman.
Appearances 25 Goals 7

Peter CARR
All of Peter's games for Motherwell came in the relegation season of 1978/79. The club was in a dreadful mess, relegation was inevitable and dramatic, and in such

circumstances Peter hardly had a chance to show his midfield talents.
Appearances 6/1 Goals 0

Joe CARSON
Signed together with Albert Kidd from Arbroath for a joint-fee of £100,000 in 1979, Joe was a towering centre half whose lanky physique and huge moustache ensured he was easily recognised. He made his debut against Airdrie on 22 December 1979 and went on to prove himself as one of Ally MacLeod's best signings for the club.

As well as being a sound defender – he had had six seasons with Arbroath – Joe was dangerous when he ventured forward and he hit his first goal against Clyde. In the promotion winning campaign of 1981/82 he missed just five games, and he was an influential performer when returning to the Premier League, scoring on the opening day of the season in a 2-2 draw with Rangers.

Joe Carson

Injury, then loss of form, restricted his appearances in the Premier League and in the 1983/84 season, which ended in relegation, big Joe managed only 20 outings and he moved to Dumbarton. From Boghead he journeyed to Partick Thistle where he enjoyed an 'Indian summer', making 101 First Division appearances for the Jags, many of them at centre forward. He finished his senior career with Stranraer and is still fondly remembered by many Motherwell supporters.
Appearances 126 Goals 8

Mark CAUGHEY
Never quite making the grade at Motherwell despite an impressive pedigree, Mark was a Northern Ireland international and a star with Linfield when Hibernian signed him. Unable to make an impression in Edinburgh, he moved to Hamilton Accies and in 21 League games there scored an excellent 13 goals. This tempted Motherwell, who released Jamie Fairlie to acquire the busy Irishman's services. However, the goals did not flow so freely at Motherwell (although he did net an own goal on his debut); indeed, they did not flow at all, and he was soon back in Northern Ireland, this time playing with Bangor.
Appearances 0/2 Goals 0

Kevin CHRISTIE
Kevin had played as a reserve at Aberdeen during Alex McLeish's latter years at Pittodrie, joining them in 1994 from Lewis United and, although he drifted to East Fife, he was remembered by Alex and recruited as a full-back. His East Fife debut was the stuff of fairytales as he scored in only 35 seconds.

Kevin Christie

Tall and gangly, the Motherwell supporters were not convinced that Kevin was a Premier League defender, and although he could knock delightful long passes with his left foot and hit a stunning shot, he never quite seemed good enough. He was allowed to join Falkirk at the tail end of the 1998/99 season, but injury consigned him to the sidelines for the first nine months of his Brockville career.
Appearances 26/3 Goals 0

Jim CLARK
Originally with Stirling Albion, Jim joined Kilmarnock in the late 1970s and became a key member of the Ayrshire club's midfield. Perhaps he was too used to Rugby Park, for he was unable to reproduce his steady form at Motherwell and left after making only a handful of outings. Signed by Motherwell in the summer of 1985, he made his debut against Clydebank early that season.
Appearances 5 Goals 0

John CLARK
The career of John Clark can be confined to a discussion of minutes rather than matches. He came on as a substitute against Albion Rovers in the promotion campaign of 1968/69.

Unfortunately, Motherwell had a settled side at the time and John could not break in. He had been signed in 1969 from Irvine Vics and was freed in 1970.
Appearances 0/1 Goals 0

Robert CLARK
In the early 1980s there were Clarks

Robert Clark

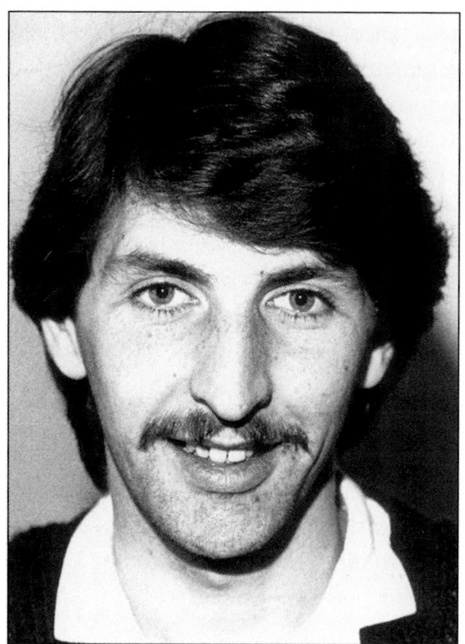

Bruce Cleland

aplenty at Kilmarnock. Indeed, so many that both Robert and Jim were able to join Motherwell briefly. Perhaps it was a pity that Motherwell never managed to secure the services of Paul Clarke, the towering centre half who was a Scotland Under-21 international. Robert arrived at Fir Park in 1984 and played as central defender or sweeper. His senior career had actually begun at Ibrox with Rangers.

Appearances 9/4 Goals 1

Bruce CLELAND

A striker who began his career with amateur side Glasgow United before moving into the junior ranks with Maryhill, Cleland's goalscoring ability quickly caught the eye of Albion Rovers. His 33 goals for the Coatbridge side in 1978/79 resulted in his transfer to Fir Park for £45,000 that summer. Unfortunately the move from part-time to full-time football had an adverse affect and he had a disastrous start with the Steelmen, scoring only twice in his first 18 games. Manager Ally MacLeod lost faith in him and it was only under David Hay's regime that he had an extended run, making 25 First Division appearances and netting 15 goals, as Motherwell won promotion to the Premier League in 1981/82. That season he also scored 12 for the reserves. Unfortunately, the following season he made just 5 Premier appearances plus 4 as a substitute before moving on.

Appearances 53/4 Goals 23

Peter CLELAND

Signed in 1951 from Newarthill Hearts, Peter could not impose his right-wing skills on the Motherwell first team scene; perhaps he was hindered by his National Service duties. He played a solitary game before moving out of Fir

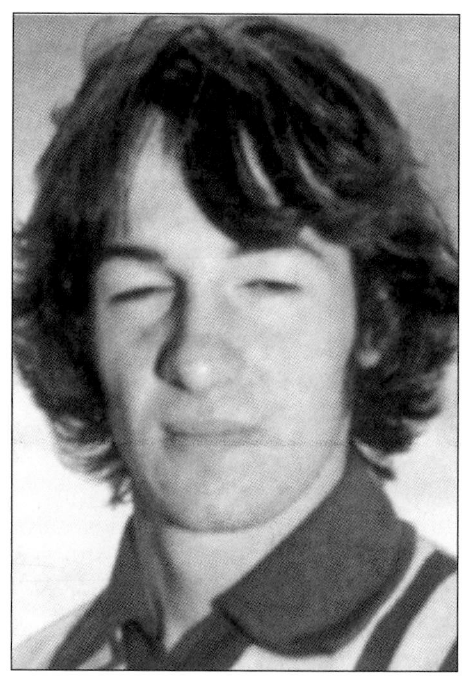

Ian Clinging

Park on a free transfer in 1953.
Appearances 1 Goals 0

Ian CLINGING
A local lad, Ian was signed from Carluke Rovers in 1977, and his bustling style and good use of the ball made him a popular figure. Whole-hearted and a great worker, Ian played 113 League games for Motherwell and contributed 21 goals. Jock Wallace tried to buy Ian while manager of Leicester City, offering £90,000, but the offer was rejected by Motherwell. Early in 1983 he joined Kilmarnock on loan, and in 1983 moved permanently to Morton. He was a solid performer at Cappielow too, before bringing down the curtain on his career at Stranraer.
Appearances 92/21 Goals 21

Tommy COAKLEY
A tricky right-winger, Coakley was something of an enigma. Capable of brilliant performances and stunning goals, he could also be anonymous and frustratingly off-form. He had previously served Glencairn Juveniles and Bellshill Athletic, but was still only sixteen when he made three appearances for the Steelmen in 1963/64; arguably he is the youngest ever Fir Park player.

He had an unusual job away from the game, as a potter. He was, however, unable to sculpt a successful career at Fir Park. Signed by Motherwell on 24 March, he made his debut just a week later, having unsuccessfully trialled with Leicester City. He was given a free transfer in 1966 and in May of that year joined Arsenal. He later played in America with Detroit, then returned to Britain to star with Morton.

Tommy made a very successful entry to senior English League management after playing and managing in English non-League football with Chelmsford, Bishop's Stortford, Hertford and Maldon. Ultimately he held the post as Walsall boss for several years in the 1980s, and he steered them into the English Second Division on a shoestring budget before returning to non-League football.
Appearances 22 Goals 1

Alfie CONN
A clever midfielder, and son of the famous Hearts player of the same name, Alfie had played with Rangers, Tottenham and Celtic amongst others before joining Motherwell in August 1981. He stayed for three years but was dreadfully hampered by injury and played only 27 League games in that time. Nevertheless, when on form he was a lovely player to watch; one of his goals against Hearts was a study in

Tommy Coakley

Alfie Conn

quality and his epic counter against East Stirling was an individual effort of the highest standard.

Born in Kirkcaldy in 1952, he joined Rangers in 1968 and was there for six years before his £140,000 move to Tottenham Hotspur. Celtic paid less than half that to sign him in 1977 and he earned great fame for having served both members of the Old Firm. Next came Pittsburg, before Hearts signed him in July 1980. By this stage he was ravaged by injury, and following a short stint with Blackpool he came to Motherwell. A clever player, he was hard to shake from the ball but ultimately too injury-prone. He won a European Cup Winners Cup medal and the full range of Scottish domestic honours.

Appearances 21/6 Goals 3

Davie COOPER

Born in Hamilton, it is fair to say Cooper was one of the most popular post-war Scottish players. His range of ball skills and sheer entertainment value made him instantly recognisable. He joined Motherwell in 1989 for £50,000, having lost his place at Rangers and seemingly nearing the end of a most successful career. It was not to be and in his twilight years at Fir Park he revealed himself to be a quite extraordinary player, whose guile and skill more than made up for advancing years.

Cooper was clearly a match-winner, a skilled craftsman and an almost unique talent. His Rangers career spanned twelve years and brought a rich array of honours. Yet, above the glittering prizes stands the memory of his cultured left-foot, his amazing dribbling, his precision crosses and his stunning dead-ball accuracy.

Davie Cooper

For Tommy McLean to have landed such a prestigious and obvious talent for only £50,000 was a real coup. Those who thought Cooper was going to Fir Park merely to play out his time were proved sorely wrong. All the wizardry and accuracy of the Cooper years at Ibrox seemed undiminished by advancing years. He was still the master of the dribble and, even more so, the weighted pass. Subtle, tricky and endearing, he was a player fans of both sides could warm to.

He won a Scottish Cup medal while at Fir Park and resurrected his international career. Of the many matches that stick out, perhaps those against Aberdeen and Dundee United in the winter of 1989 were the finest. Tragically, Davie died shortly after leaving Motherwell to return to his first club, Clydebank. It is no exaggeration to say that the Scottish nation was both stunned and deeply saddened by his untimely death.
Appearances 157 Goals 17

Mike CORMACK
A young midfielder who was brought to the club from Highland League football, the former Deveronvale youngster made 17 outings for Motherwell and netted one goal. He joined Kilmarnock in 1984.
Appearances 6/11 Goals 1

Martyn CORRIGAN
Falkirk's talented young full-back was always going to be highly-sought after, given that he had pace, drive and a cool head. It was Motherwell who snapped him up in the summer of 1999 and instantly solved their right-back problem.

He made his debut as a substitute away to St Johnstone, and was given an instant example of what Motherwell expected as the other full-back Stephen McMillan scored for Motherwell that day. Corrigan lived up to early expectations and, ironically enough, he scored against St Johnstone the next time Motherwell played them!
Appearances 18(1) Goals 1

Stevie Cowan

Stevie COWAN
A popular striker who came to Motherwell in 1987 from Hibernian. His debut was almost sensational as he scored against St Mirren within 15 minutes, but the goal was disallowed. However, there were plenty more to come and he was a regular marksman for Motherwell. He was a good goalscorer, but sadly only stayed at Fir Park for two seasons before leaving. He later starred in Irish football and Portadown were amongst those to benefit from his goalscoring prowess.

His career had started with St Mirren under Alex Ferguson. He followed Fergie to Aberdeen, where he was a fringe striker, before moving to Hibernian where the goals arrived thick and fast.
Appearances 44/7 Goals 11

Willie COWIE
Signed in 1956 from Kilsyth Rangers, Willie was very much the traditional tall centre half. He could not displace the mercurial Andy Paton and left Motherwell after three seasons on a free transfer to Queen of the South.
Appearances 10 Goals 0

Charlie COX
A cultured wing-half, Charlie joined Motherwell from Hearts in December 1951 and within six months had helped The Steelmen win the Scottish Cup. Signed for £6,500 along with Tommy Sloan, Charlie was a dedicated and meticulous player who linked defence and attack with considerable skill.

He started his football career with Dumbarton Academy and captained the side that won the Dumbarton League Shield. He then joined Yoker Juniors but such was his talent that he was snapped up by Hearts in May 1944. He was a part-timer at Tynecastle, and ultimately this led to his departure on Boxing Day 1951, but not before he scored a remarkable winner against Rangers while reduced to the status of 'passenger' out on the wing with a bad leg knock.

Together with Tommy Sloan he settled in quickly at Motherwell and helped continue the offside-trap that served The Steelmen well in the 1940s and '50s. In the 1952 Scottish Cup final he controlled Dundee's record signing Billy Steel as Motherwell romped home 4-0. A year later he was in the team that was relegated. However, his experience was crucial to the side's immediate 'B' Division title win.

A useful cricketer, he played 89 League games for Motherwell and scored 4 times; he also scored 4 Scottish Cup goals, one of them the last gasp equaliser in an unforgettable 5-5 draw at Pittodrie. The Scottish Cup, it seemed, always brought the best out of Charlie.
Appearances 89 Goals 4

Owen COYLE
Born in Paisley, Owen was signed by Alex McLeish in January 1997 and in just over two years at the club was a prolific marksman and popular figure. When he left the club it was to join First Division Dunfermline Athletic and he almost instantly helped them regain their Premier League status.

Charlie Cox

Owen started his senior career in 1985/86 with Dumbarton. He was to stay with the Sons for just over three seasons, playing for the Republic of Ireland Under-21s against Scotland at Easter Road in February 1987 and scoring their only goal in a 1-4 defeat. He thrived at Boghead and scored 36 League goals in 100 starts. That strike-ratio earned him a £25,000 move along the road to Clydebank where he was seldom out of the goals. Indeed, in his first season he scored 16 times in 36 League starts. In just two seasons at Kilbowie he hit 33 goals in 63 games. A goal every other game made several managers interested and it was Airdrie's Alex MacDonald, with a club record £175,000 fee, who took the plunge.

Owen ended the 1989/90 season as the top goalscorer in Scotland, with a haul of 27 League counters from his stints with Airdrie and Bankies. It would have been difficult to better the start Owen made with the Diamonds, for he scored 10 times in his first 10 games. In 1993 Bolton Wanderers stepped in and Owen was fortunate to contribute to a period of re-birth there; Wanderers built an awesome cup reputation and battled their way into the Premiership. His personal reward was a full cap for the Republic of Ireland in 1994.

In October 1995 he joined Dundee United in a £400,000 deal and helped them return to the top flight. After 43 games in Tangerine, and 11 goals, he joined Motherwell in a deal that saw Jamie Dolan heading for Tayside.

Appearances 77 Goals 23

Owen Coyle

Brian COYNE

Born in Glasgow in December 1959, Brian was called up by Celtic from St Rochs when only seventeen. He made his debut for Celtic soon afterwards, but broke his ankle later that season and was unable to sustain the breakthrough at Parkhead. He took his midfield talents to Shrewsbury Town in June 1979, but made only one outing for the Shrews before joining Motherwell.

He fared better at Motherwell and won a First Division Championship medal in 1982. Nevertheless he made only 35 outings before leaving the club. He later served Worcester City as a player and Newtown of Wales as a player/manager.

Appearances 27/8 Goals 2

Tommy COYNE

The first Motherwell player ever to be capped by the Republic of Ireland, Tommy was one of the most prolific marksmen of his generation. He first sprang to prominence with Clydebank

Tommy Coyne

and then had spells with both Dundee clubs, making a huge impression with Dundee, bagging over 30 goals in one season. From Dundee he moved to Celtic for £500,000 and, despite an excellent record there, he was surprisingly allowed to drift out of Parkhead into English football with Tranmere Rovers.

Motherwell signed Coyne from Tranmere for £125,000. He topped the Motherwell scoring charts and furthered his international career with the Republic of Ireland, playing in the 1994 World Cup finals in America. Nicknamed 'The Cobra' due to his lightning reflexes, he was a marvellous goal predator and formed a wonderful partnership with both Dougie Arnott and Owen Coyle. At Motherwell he was a reliable scorer and had many purple patches. A personal favourite of his was the goal that enabled Motherwell to beat Celtic 1-0 in the third round of the Scottish Cup in January 1994. When he eventually moved away from Motherwell it was to rejoin Dundee, but his spell there could never match his first period and he was allowed to join Falkirk on loan at one stage.

Appearances 132 Goals 59

Stephen CRAIGAN

From Comber in County Down, Stephen had Northern Irish League experience with Bangor before joining Motherwell, who initially sent him to Blantyre Vics before calling him up in the summer of 1995. He immediately went to Switzerland with the Fir Park youth team which went on to reach the final of the tournament, only to be beaten by Real Madrid. Unfortunately, Stephen was unable to make a central defensive berth his own in the face of talented competition. However, he gave Motherwell five seasons of loyal service before being released in the summer of 2000 and joining Partick Thistle.

Appearances 29 Goals 0

Stephen Craigan

Richard CUMMING

In 1950 Motherwell went to Killermont Amateurs to recruit inside forward Cumming. He was to stay at Fir Park for just two years and in that time managed only 2 League outings. His next port of call was Dumbarton.

Appearances 2 Goals 0

Dennis CUNNINGHAM

An inside forward who played only a single game for Motherwell, Dennis was signed from Hearts in 1961. He was freed within twelve months. That single outing came at St Johnstone's Muirton Park in a 1-1 draw.

Appearances 1 Goals 0

Sasa CURCIC

Controversially signed towards the end of the 1999/2000 season, Sasa arrived at Fir Park with mixed baggage. He was the player who had 14 full caps for Yugoslavia, and had joined Aston Villa for £4 million less than three years previously, but slipped into a downward spiral.

His appearances for Motherwell were few and disappointing. Born in Belgrade, he had played with OFK Belgrade, Partizan Belgrade then Bolton Wanderers, Aston Villa and Crystal Palace before joining Motherwell in March 2000. It was said the presence of Miodrag Krivokapic on the Fir Park coaching staff was a big factor in Sasa agreeing to come to Motherwell.

He was released by Motherwell at the end of the 1999/2000 season, part of a nine-player clear out. Remarkably, he was only twenty-eight at the time and clearly an unfulfilled talent. He was noticeable as much for the white boots he wore as any other factor on the field.

Appearances 3(3) Goals 0

Nick CUSACK

A centre forward, Nick was signed by Tommy McLean in 1989 from Peterborough United for £50,000. Prior to the Posh he had been with Alvechurch and Leicester City, as well as studying for a degree. Tall and athletic, he could score with both head and feet, but within months encountered disciplinary woe. He was sent off against both Hearts and Aberdeen and there is no doubt his brushes with authority hastened his departure from Scotland. His problem lay not so much in an aggressive manner but rather an ungainly style that often saw him going for high balls with his elbows dangerously positioned.

He later played with Darlington and Oxford United as well as Fulham, scoring a presentable amount of goals at each club. As the millennium neared he was playing with Swansea.

Appearances 68 Goals 18

Nick Cusack

D

Vic DAVIDSON

A talented midfielder, Vic was one of the Celtic band of reserves known as the 'Quality Street Kids', and played alongside the likes of Kenny Dalglish and Lou Macari at Parkhead. He was surprisingly freed by Celtic in June 1975 and Motherwell had his considerable skills at their disposal for three years. He scored 19 times in 88 League games and was always able to raise his game against Celtic. Vic later played with Blackpool in the English League before settling in the United States. Whilst a Motherwell player he joined the elite band of Steelmen to have scored 5 times in a senior match, the occasion being an Anglo-Scottish Cup tie against Alloa which Motherwell won 7-0.

Appearances 88 Goals 19

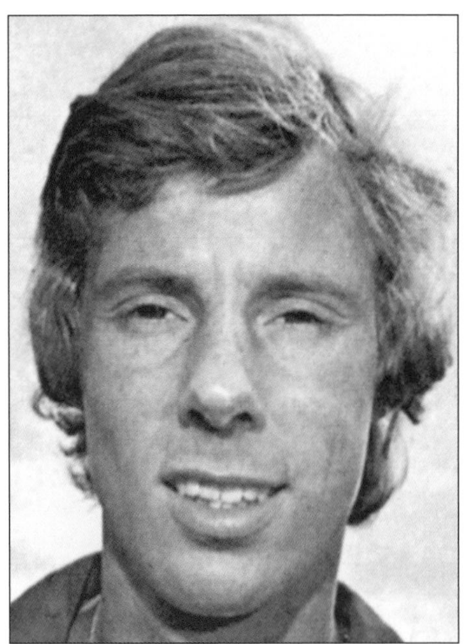

Vic Davidson

Billy Davies

Billy DAVIES

No one at Motherwell could have imagined in 1994 that Alex McLeish was signing a man who would one day be Motherwell manager. Davies had been a workman-like midfielder, whose busy style and neat play allied to an attacking bent made him a useful player.

Davies was a good buy for Motherwell and it was noticeable that when he fell out of Alex McLeish's plans, Motherwell struggled. He only just stayed at Fir Park in the Harri Kampman years, turning down the chance to join Morton. However, his patience and loyalty were well rewarded when he was appointed manager shortly after the departure of Harri Kampman.

Davies worked well with chairman John Boyle and chief executive Pat Nevin and gradually built a side capable of exciting play and adventurous attacking. Signed in March 1994 from Dunfermline Athletic for £50,000, he must rank as one of the club's best buys.

Appearances 116 Goals 9

John DAVIES

Signed by his brother Billy, John came to Fir Park having proved himself to be one of the more consistent midfielders in the Scottish game. His career began at Clydebank before he tried his luck in Sweden. Here the tale of two brothers really caught the eye. Billy had been playing with Jonkoping when he moved up a division to Elfsborg. On his departure from Jonkoping he suggested that his brother John would be an ideal replacement. The deal was done, and then, as luck would have it, Jonkoping drew Elfsborg out of the hat in the Swedish Cup. Inevitably, John's side won!

When he came back to Scotland it was a return to Clydebank, and he made over 100 appearances for them before St Johnstone offered a £165,000 cheque. He thrived in the Saints side and then went on to play with Airdrie and Ayr United, before Billy decided he would be an ideal squad player to have at Fir Park. In truth, the move to Premier Division Motherwell probably came a couple of years too late for him to have maximum impact.

Appearances 7(1) Goals 0

George DAWSON

A wiry, bustling, inside forward, George was recruited from Rutherglen Glencairn in 1952, and played with Motherwell for almost 3 seasons. He had a difficult task breaking into a side that had just won the cup but he never let the club down when needed. George was in the Motherwell side which won the Lord Provost of Glasgow's Trophy on 22 September 1952, beating Hibs 5-1 in a Cup winners against League champions match. He also scored a goal in that match. Eventually, after 15 matches and 2 goals, he decided to seek first team football and gained a free transfer in 1955. London, and particularly QPR, attracted him, but he played only a single match for the R's, in 1955.

Appearances 15 Goals 2

John 'Dixie' DEANS

Following the departure of Joe McBride to Celtic in June 1965, there was a void at the centre of Motherwell's attack. The gap was finally filled when Bobby Howitt signed John Deans from Neilston Juniors in October 1965 for a mere £100. Deans' exploits in junior football had earned him the nickname 'Dixie', after the great Everton striker, and by the time he left Fir Park (ironically following McBride to Celtic) the stocky forward had earned himself a place in the hearts of most Motherwell supporters.

John came to prominence as a prolific goalscorer with Neilston, and when he amassed a staggering 60 goals in one season, Motherwell moved to pip Newcastle United for his signature.

Deans was an enthusiastic marksman and very popular player who brought vigour and energy to his role as centre forward. Although only 5 ft 7in, he was excellent in the air and powerful on the deck. He made his League debut at Kilmarnock in March 1966 and in the following season broke the club's post-war goalscoring record by netting 30 League goals. In the reserves his goals

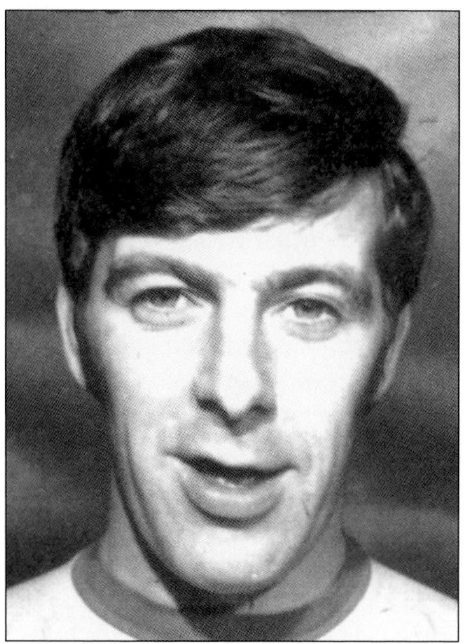

John Deans

had helped secure a Second Eleven cup final spot, and now his exploits had paved the way for promotion. Unfortunately, however, controversy continually shadowed his Fir Park career.

Not long after his first hat-trick, against Dunfermline, he was sent-off against Celtic in December 1966 and thus began a trail of clashes with authority. Sendings-off against Dunfermline, Aberdeen, Clyde, Hamilton and Stoke City followed. As the catalogue of dismissals grew, he became increasingly despondent about his future at Fir Park, given his growing bad reputation.

He was sold to Celtic in October 1971 and Jock Stein was pleased to have secured his services for a meagre £17,500 – less than he paid for McBride four years earlier, although 'Dixie' was serving a six week suspension at the time. Deans enjoyed a prolific career with Celtic, particularly when they met Hibernian, netting a hat-trick in the 6-1 mauling of the luckless Hibees in the 1972 Scottish Cup final. He also scored the goal that clinched the League at Easter Road in 1973 and another hat-trick in the 6-3 League Cup final triumph over Hibs in 1974. He scored six goals in a match against Partick Thistle when Celtic ran up a 7-0 win.

It was not all roses for Deans at Parkhead, however, and he was amongst the earliest victims of penalty shoot-outs, missing a penalty in a European Cup semi-final tie against Inter Milan. He did nonetheless secure every domestic honour with the Celts and was twice capped by Scotland, against East Germany and Spain

He had been Bobby Howitt's first signing after his move from coaching at Morton, and arguably his finest.

Appearances 152 Goals 78

Pat DELANEY

Signed as an eighteen-year-old in December 1958 from Douglas Water Thistle, he developed into a fine player, capable of playing orthodox full-back, pivot or even as a free scoring centre forward. He was from genuine football stock, and his father Jimmy played for both Celtic and Manchester United as well as Falkirk, Derry City and Cork.

Pat made his first team debut as a centre half against St Mirren in 1959, played in 1960/61 as a right-back, then ran riot as a centre forward in 1961/62, scoring three League hat-tricks in just eight weeks. Yet he quickly gained 3 Under-23 caps as a full-back and defence was probably his best position.

In 1965 Pat scored twice for Motherwell in the Summer Cup final win over Dundee United, having assumed the captaincy

Pat Delaney

from Bert McCann. Indeed he was the hero of the Summer Cup run, netting 8 times in the 10 matches required to land the silverware.

Delaney was sold by Bobby Howitt to Dunfermline in October 1966 for £17,000, and went on to play in several European ties for the Pars. He later played for Clyde and Airdrie.

Appearances 158 Goals 21

Jim DEMPSEY

Signed in 1978 from Lanark United, Jim was a defender who made 20 League appearances for the club. Ultimately he was given a free transfer after two years at Fir Park, and he went on to become a very loyal servant to Clyde. He later served Falkirk, from 1984, but it was with the Bully Wee that he made his reputation as a solid, if unspectacular, performer.

Appearances 20 Goals 0

Greig DENHAM

Cruciate ligament injuries are amongst the worst a player can suffer and Greig was struck down in 1998 with this curse. At that point he had been breaking into the first team in his role as centre half.

He broke back into the side under Billy Davies but, with experienced central defenders like Teale, Kemble and then Strong in the picture, his options were restricted. He moved to Falkirk in May 2000 as the Brockville club sought to build a side capable of escaping the First Division, and teamed up with former team-mate Kevin Christie.

Appearances 47 Goals 0

Billy DICKSON

Like Jim Dempsey, Billy Dickson was to make his name away from Fir Park. But whereas Jim made his reputation after leaving Motherwell, it was the opposite for Billy. He was a stalwart at Kilmarnock

Greig Denham

Michel Doesburg

and already a Scotland international when he joined Motherwell in 1974. Alas, his move to Motherwell did not work out and he was to make only 12 outings for The Steelmen.

Appearances 10/2 Goals 0

Jim DOBBIN

Dobbin is yet another who flourished when away from Motherwell. Born in Dunfermline in 1963, Jim joined Celtic from Whitburn BC and made only two outings for the Celts before joining Motherwell on loan for two League games in 1983/84. He then returned to Parkhead, only to be sold to Doncaster Rovers. He settled well in South Yorkshire and five seasons on joined Barnsley, before later moving to Grimsby Town. At each club he played with a great passion that would surely have been an asset to Motherwell.

Appearances 1/1 Goals 0

Michel DOESBURG

Signed in 1998 from AZ Alkmaar, Michel was a solid, hard working full-back. Like so many Dutch players his strength was his comfort on the ball and his excellent and intelligent distribution. He had played with Heerenveen, Wageningen, Haarlem and Beverwyk in Holland. Although initially he looked like the answer to any full-back questions, he gradually slipped from favour and in the spring of 2000 was moved on to First Division Dunfermline Athletic.

Appearances 51 Goals 0

Jamie DOLAN

Signed in 1987 from Motherwell BC, this Salsburgh-born youngster became a midfield dynamo for Motherwell. Originally basing much of his game on a high work rate and tiger-like tackling, he gradually evolved into a very capable schemer. Arguably his big break at Fir Park was the departure of Colin O'Neill through injury in 1991.

Like many players in similar circumstances, he found himself initially stereotyped and had to endure a long wait before others recognised his skilful qualities. For all his crunching midfield displays, his Fir Park touchstone was probably his display in goal in 1996 against Celtic. The match was an epic. Motherwell led 1-0 then lost 'keeper Howie with a broken jaw. Jamie took over in goal and kept Celtic at bay, until eventually Hay equalised. However, the day had a happy ending with Ian Ross scoring in the dying seconds for a memorable 2-1 win

One man who did know of his skills was Tommy McLean, who took him to Dundee United early in 1997, with Owen Coyle and £75,000 heading to Fir Park

Jamie Dolan

in exchange. From Dundee United he moved on to Dunfermline Athletic and then Livingston. Jamie still visits Fir Park when not playing.
Appearances 194 Goals 5

Frank DONNACHIE
A 1964 signing from Shotts Bon Accord, Frank stayed with Motherwell until 1967 and his eventual departure to Stenhousemuir. He played 9 games for Motherwell and scored a solitary goal, in a 1-3 defeat at Dundee United.
Appearances 9 Goals 1

John DONNELLY
Signed in 1979 from Notts County, John was a midfielder who lasted only one year at Motherwell. His 25 League games brought two goals, but his move to Dumbarton in 1980 brought in a useful £25,000. John served the Sons well and scored quite a few more than the expected quota at Boghead.
Appearances 21/4 Goals 2

Tom DONNELLY
An ex-Rangers midfielder who joined Motherwell in 1967 after being granted a free transfer by the Ibrox club, Tom Donnelly settled well at Fir Park, and his subtle promptings created several goals for the likes of 'Dixie' Deans. A university student, he took great pleasure in scoring against Rangers in a keenly fought 2-2 draw in 1969. He left in 1971 to join East Stirlingshire.
Appearances 70/2 Goals 10

Tom Donnelly

Andy Dornan

Andy DORNAN

Dornan was a powerful and clever full-back who made 92 League appearances for Motherwell before moving on to England with Walsall. Andy was snapped up from Alex Ferguson's Aberdeen in December 1982, and made a brilliant debut in a 2-0 win at Kilmarnock; thereafter he was a regular in the number 2 jersey and was the frequent subject of transfer speculation.

After four seasons at Fir Park his game became a little stale and he was allowed to move to Walsall, where he proved a very popular player. He did return to Scotland in the 1990s, plying his trade back in his native north-east with Montrose, who were relegated from the First Division at the end of the 1991/92 season.

Appearances 92 Goals 4

Mario DORNER

Dorner was signed in 1997 from VfB Modling, although technically he was out of contract at the time. A bustling centre forward, he showed up well for Motherwell, but was unable to hold down a first team place and was eventually allowed to leave without ever signing permanently. His previous clubs had included FC Linz, FC Kreams, and Admira Wacker. He had 11 Under-21 caps for Austria as well as 14 at Under-18 level and 8 Olympic caps. He later played with Darlington in England.

Appearances 1/1 Goals 0

Jamie DOYLE

A talented midfielder with Partick Thistle, Jamie never quite shone as brightly for Motherwell. This was a pity, as he had industry and heart enough, but apparently did not fit into the Motherwell scheme of things. Signed in 1984, he left in 1987.

Appearances 35/2 Goals 1

Jamie Doyle

Cammy DUNCAN
So useful a young 'keeper was Cammy that he took the road south as a youngster, but found openings at Sunderland limited. It was from there that Tommy McLean recruited him, and in truth he was a good goalkeeper. However, after two years at Fir Park he began to lose out to the likes of Ally Maxwell, and thus he moved on. He was sold to Partick Thistle in 1989 for the not inconsiderable sum of £60,000. He later made a name for himself with Ayr United, whom he joined in a swap deal for Sammy Johnston in March 1991. He was released by Ayr at the end of the 1995/96 season but was still playing senior football in November 1996, this time with Albion Rovers.
Appearances 60 Goals 0

Sieb DYKSTRA
A commanding goalkeeper, Sieb was signed by Tommy McLean in August 1991

Cammy Duncan

Sieb Dykstra

from Hasselt KSC, a small Dutch side. He soon established himself as a Fir Park favourite – anything within the box, or even near it, was fair game for this extrovert. He left on the eve of Alex McLeish's arrival at the club in July 1994 and joined QPR for £350,000. Life with the Londoners was not all that Sieb had hoped for and he spent periods on loan with Bristol Rovers and Wycombe Wanderers before Tommy, by now the manager of Dundee United, signed him again. Although perhaps not the greatest goalkeeper in the history of Motherwell, he was surely one of the most popular and charismatic.

Appearances 80 Goals 0

E

Johannes EDVALDSSON
Edvaldsson was a rarity in that he was an Icelandic international at a time

when Motherwell did not sign players of such quality. 'Shuggie', as he was affectionately known, joined The Steelmen during the twilight of his career in August 1982 when he was lured by Jock Wallace from German side Hanover. There were only 1,079 present to see his debut against little Forfar in the League Cup and his League debut came against Rangers in a 2-2 draw a few days later.

Edvaldsson completed his first season with 35 appearances and 2 goals – the first of which came up at Aberdeen. Prior to playing with Hanover he had served Valur and, most famously, Celtic. A determined individual, he was an uncompromising defender and a valuable addition up front at set pieces. In April 1984 Johannes was freed by Motherwell.

Appearances 55 Goals 6

Johannes Edvaldsson

Roy ESSANDOH

A young Irish striker, Roy made a few outings under Alex McLeish. He was noticeable, standing as he did at 6 ft 2 in and being amongst the few black players in the Scottish Premier League at that time. Signed in 1995, along with Stephen Craigan, he came to Fir Park from Belfast club Glentoran.

Appearances 0/4 Goals 0

F

Jamie FAIRLIE

Jamie was a Hamilton Accies legend, who joined Motherwell too late to make a mark. A wonderful attacking midfielder, he joined Accies in June 1974 from Calderbank BC. Silky, creative and strong, he had all the attributes of a top class player and the wonder was that he did not move to a bigger club earlier. He actually joined Motherwell in 1987 from Clydebank, and played only a dozen games for Motherwell before returning to his beloved Accies the same year.

There was, however, one golden moment in that short career. In the Skol Cup quarter final of 1987, Fairlie scored the only goal in a 1-0 win over Hibernian that sent Motherwell into the semi-finals. In truth he would probably have been happiest being a one-club man. A Scotland 'B' international while at Accies, he recovered from dreadful injuries sustained at Falkirk in March 1981 to continue his career.

Appearances 8/4 Goals 1

Willie FALCONER

Tall strikers with a panache for goalscoring are always most welcome. When, as in the case of Willie Falconer, they arrive and promptly save you from relegation, they become even more popular!

Born in Aberdeen, Willie began his career with Alex Ferguson's Aberdeen and had been a team-mate of Alex McLeish. The latter fact would ultimately serve Motherwell to good effect. From Aberdeen, Falconer moved to England, and carved out a useful career with Sheffield United, Watford and Middlesbrough. A move back north of the border to Celtic brought him a Scottish Cup winner's badge and this enticed Motherwell to snap him up when a bad run threatened their Premier Division status. It was a huge mistake to let him go with Tommy Coyne and Shaun McSkimming to Dundee in the summer of 1998.

Willie Falconer

Jamie Fairlie

The proverbial 'barrowload' of goals followed for Dundee, and clearly Motherwell had let a quality performer slip through their fingers.

Appearances 58 Goals 10

John FALLON

A goalkeeper who had made his name with Celtic, John came to Motherwell during a goalkeeping crisis in the 1971/72 season. He gave a superb display against Rangers in the Scottish Cup replay at Ibrox that convinced many Motherwell supporters that he had exacerbated that crisis.

One good story surrounds John's spell at Motherwell. East Fife, requiring a point from their game at Fir Park on

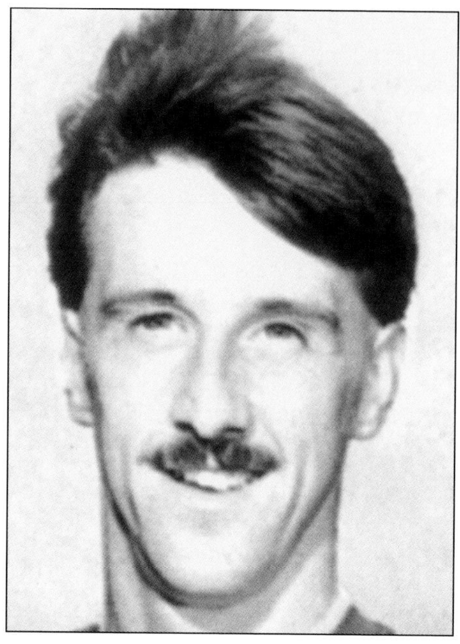

Ray Farningham

29 April to avoid relegation, were offered a colour television each if they could stay up. They duly got the point they desired, and after the game Motherwell captain Bobby Watson suggested in the Motherwell dressing room that 'instead of going out tonight we could all go round to John's house and watch his colour telly'. Fallon responded 'What? There's no point, I don't have a colour telly'. Back came Watson with the killer line: 'But I thought East Fife promised everyone who helped them stay up a colour telly!'

Appearances 10 Goals 0

Ray FARNINGHAM

A slim, cultured midfielder, Ray spent several years with lowly Forfar Athletic, learning his trade. In 1982 he helped the Loons reach the Scottish Cup semi-finals, and the one-time Dundee United player's form was consistency itself. He improved year on year, and when Motherwell signed him in 1986 for £12,000 they pipped a number of interested parties. A wonderful worker, he gave the club solid service and scored a good number of goals, including 6 Premier counters in the 1987/88 season. Ray's most famous game in Motherwell's colours came in November 1986, when he scored the only goal in a 1-0 win at Rangers.

For reasons that were never very clear, he was allowed to move to Dunfermline for £50,000 in 1989, at a time when he was growing in stature. From Dunfermline he drifted around the lower reaches of the game, enjoying a fairly lengthy spell at Dundee.

Appearances 69/7 Goals 12

Isaac FARRELL

A midfielder, Isaac played in the opening game of the 1976/77 season against Kilmarnock. The match ended as a 1-1 draw, and that was his only appearance for the club. He was signed from Rangers in 1975 and had three outings as a substitute in the League Cup campaign that followed. The following season he had two League Cup ties as well as that one League match under his belt.

Appearances 1 Goals 0

Iain FERGUSON

Despite learning his trade with Fir Park BC in the late 1970s, Iain did not join Motherwell until December 1990. As a youngster Iain caught Dundee's eye and his good form there earned him a lucrative move to Rangers. He did reasonably well at Ibrox, but was allowed to join Dundee United in 1986. He was a prolific marksman for the Tangerines and scored the winning goal in their remarkable UEFA Cup win at Barcelona's Nou Camp Stadium. Next came a move to Hearts where he scored another memorable European goal, this time against Bayern Munich.

Tommy McLean signed him for Motherwell for £100,000 in December 1990. Although never terribly consistent, he wrote off any faults by scoring the opening goal in the 1991 Scottish Cup final win over Dundee United. Ferguson moved to Airdrie in September 1993 and then played with Portadown and Dundee.

Appearances 34/17 Goals 10

Bobby FLAVELL

Having played in the lower English Leagues with Burnley, Halifax, Chesterfield and Burnley, Bobby then played in Sweden with Vastear Haninge before joining Hibernian in 1981. He came to Motherwell twelve months later, as part of the deal that took the much-loved Willie Irvine to Easter Road. Bobby never commanded a regular spot at Fir Park, although he bagged his fair share of goals when he did play. He moved out on a free transfer to Dundee United, before ending his senior career at Berwick Rangers.

Iain Ferguson

Bobby Flavell

Appearances 27/4 Goals 6

Graeme FORBES

Long-haired, muscular and with a hint of 'Roy of the Rovers' about him, Graeme Forbes was the kind of player who won approval from the fans for his sheer commitment. Experiencing both relegation and promotion with the club, he appeared to play with a passion regardless of the occasion.

Born in Forfar in 1958, he joined Motherwell from Lochee United in 1980. Although viewed as a centre half, he had enough skill and strength to play in

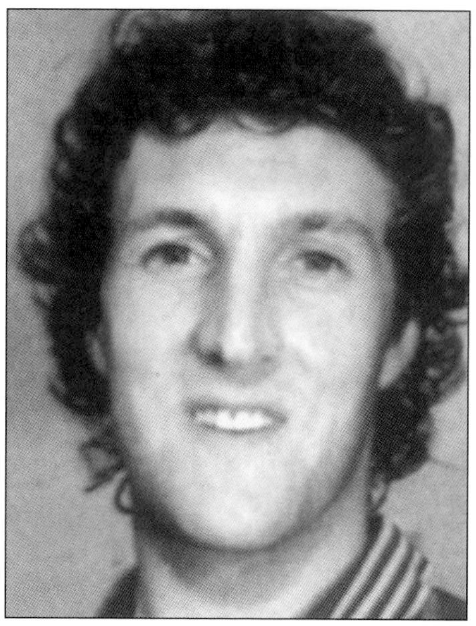

Graeme Forbes

midfield. Perhaps the most immediately impressive aspect of his play was his ability to score frequently. Ironically, the only season in which he failed to score ended with his move. However, such was the club's perilous financial position that Tommy McLean may have been motivated by pressure to generate income rather than by any assessment of Graeme's worth. Being sold when aged twenty-eight and at the peak of his powers hardly suggests a transfer the club really desired.

In September 1986 he moved to Walsall, who were not exactly leading lights in English football, for £80,000. Nevertheless, he made the move to England with ease and in just four seasons amassed 173 League outings. The Midlands side were as impressed with his commitment as the Fir Park faithful had been and he proved a most popular figure with his new club.

Appearances 169/16 Goals 16

Jim FORREST

Not to be confused with the free-scoring centre forward of the same name who starred with Rangers, this Jim was a tall inside forward with an eye for goals. At his peak he was a dangerous player, as his international cap against England in 1958 suggests.

Signed from Newarthill Hearts in 1949, he made his debut at the tail end of the 1949/50 season and scored a brace in his second game, against Stirling Albion. The very next season he scored 27 goals in 45 matches and he and his striking partner, Archie Kelly, did not miss a single game, League or cup.

When Motherwell won the 'B' Division in 1954 he played in every match but failed to score in the 12-1 thumping of Dundee United. Jim had a nightmare in his only Scotland appearance and there

Jim Forrest

were those who suggested it badly dented his confidence. Granted a free transfer in 1960, he joined Stenhousemuir. A versatile chap, he had also played at full-back and wing-half during his stint at Motherwell.

Appearances 215 Goals 58

Alex FORSYTH

Alex's best days were behind him when he joined Motherwell. This was a pity as he had been a notable full-back in his prime. He started with Arsenal but made his mark at Partick Thistle in 1968. In his time at Firhill he certainly made his mark against Motherwell, being a goalscorer for the Jags in their 8-3 thrashing of Motherwell in December 1971. Alex won a League Cup winner's badge there before moving to Manchester United for £100,000. After his distinguished career at Old Trafford and in the Scotland side, he joined Rangers on loan and then Motherwell. But his pace and strength were on the wane by the time he joined Motherwell and he made only a handful of outings. He moved to Hamilton Accies in 1983.

Appearances 18/1 Goals 0

Tom FORSYTH

While with Motherwell Tom was either an inside forward or a wing-half. He was talented, strong and determined to succeed. Signed in 1967 from Stonehouse Violet, he spent five years at Fir Park and won the first of his Scotland caps, against Denmark, while a Motherwell player. After rattling up 150 League games he was sold to Rangers in October 1972.

He was always going to be a hard player to replace. His drive and fitness were superb, and nothing seemed to intimidate him, Ibrox and Celtic Park holding no fears. Youngsters with that kind of talent are hard to hold on to, and when they can combine skill with aggression they are even more highly sought after.

He became something of a Rangers legend. A complete defender, he rarely ventured forward, but in the one hundredth Scottish Cup final, ironically enough an Old Firm final, he scored the winning goal. He was part of Rangers treble-winning side in 1976 and a stalwart at the heart of Scotland's defence, although manager Tommy Docherty once labelled him famously 'a carthorse'. Ally MacLeod had more faith in Tom and he played in all three Scotland games in the 1978 World Cup finals in Argentina.

Tom later coached and managed Dunfermline and then joined his good friend Tommy McLean at Motherwell. When McLean moved to Hearts, Tom

Alex Forsyth

Tom Forsyth

went with him and that was to be his last post in senior Scottish football.

Appearances 150 Goals 17

Gary FRASER

A small, wiry midfield player, Gary was signed from Queen's Park in the summer of 1986. He started the League game with Dundee on 27 January 1987 but also was listed 9 times as substitute that term. In 1987/88 he had 8 League appearances and was listed as substitute 7 times. While he appeared in early season friendlies the following season, he did not feature again and was freed in 1988.
Apperances 8/16 Goals 0

Paul FRYER

Paul made his debut in a 0-4 reversal at Celtic, during a season in which Motherwell finished bottom of the Premier League. He was a substitute the following week against Dundee, but that was the total extent of his Fir Park career. He was signed from Rotherham on loan in 1983, but was a Scotland Youth cap and might have been worth a gamble. He could list Leicester City, Rotherham, Charlton, Northampton and Aldershot amongst his footballing employers.
Appearances 1/1 Goals 0

John GAHAGAN

A wonderfully gifted winger, Gahagan was slightly built but marvellously tricky and a constant source of entertainment. His career started with Clydebank, but it was only after he reverted to the junior ranks with Shettleston that he caught Motherwell's attention. While playing in a Junior League Cup final at Fir Park, Motherwell boss Ally MacLeod was so taken by Gahagan that he signed him. That was in December 1979 and he made his debut against Airdrie later that month.

He stayed for eleven years, winning a First Division championship medal in Davie Hay's all-conquering 1982 side, and repeating the feat in Tommy McLean's side of 1985. He became a firm favourite with the fans, who honoured him with his own song – 'Johnny Gahagan On The Wing'! When he left Motherwell it was to join Morton in 1990 and, ironically enough, he soon found himself playing against Motherwell in the Scottish cup quarter-finals. The tie was eventually won by Motherwell on penalties but only after

John Gahagan

Gahagan's goal had earned Morton a 1-1 replay draw at Cappielow. If any player deserved to win a Scottish Cup medal with Motherwell it was surely Gahagan.

One interesting footnote on Gahagan's career must be the number of substitute appearances he made for the club ... no player can match his 93 outings from the bench!

Appearances 198/93 Goals 38

William GALLACHER

Signed in 1961 from Blantyre Victoria, this full-back was something of an enigma. He played in four games and contrived to score twice in that time, a better ratio than many big name strikers. However, he left after his quartet of League outings. It should be said that he scored both goals in a 4-0 win over St Mirren in 1965, a full four years after joining Motherwell.

Appearances 4 Goals 2

Eric GARCIN

Born in Lille, France, Eric was signed in November 1997 from Toulouse. Tall and slim, he was a skilful midfielder whose best moment at Fir Park came in the 6-2 win over Hibernian, Eric capping a great fightback with Motherwell's third goal directly from a free-kick. He had played with Le Mans, Nîmes and Avignon in France, and was once a team-mate of Eric Cantona at Nîmes. Unable to impose himself at Fir Park, he moved to Dundee but was even less successful at Dens Park.

Appearances 7/4 Goals 1

Ian GARDINER

Bobby Ancell's first major buy, Ian hailed from Balbeggie and joined Motherwell from East Fife in 1955. He had made his Bayview bow in 1949/50 when the

Eric Garcin

Ian Gardiner

Fifers, with the remarkable Charlie 'Legs' Fleming, were an excellent attacking side and he went on to gain a Scottish League cap against the Irish League in 1954/55. At Fir Park he joined that elite band of players who have scored on their debut when he netted in a 2-2 draw with Celtic. A week later he scored another at Queen of the South.

A tall centre at 5 ft 11 in, he was an uneasy member of the Ancell scene as his physical build made him stand apart. Ancell quickly developed a preference for small and thoughtful players whereas Gardiner was all about strength and work-rate. Nevertheless, his debut proved he had finishing ability and he went on to give valuable service. He hit a splendid hat-trick against Airdrie early in the 1956/57 season and another a few weeks later against Queen of the South. If proof of his success were needed it came in November 1957, when he gained a Scotland cap against Wales at Hampden.

However, the ascendancy of the 'Babes' and the 'pocket dynamo' figures like Reid, Weir, Hunter, Quinn and St John signalled the end for Gardiner and he was sold to Raith Rovers for £1,500 on 10 January, 1959. He later served St Johnstone.

Appearances 95 Goals 47

John GARDINER

A Highland-born goalkeeper who was recruited from Dundee United for £10,000 in 1984, he made 78 outings, but was unable to keep Ally Maxwell from the number 1 jersey and was freed in 1987. He later managed successfully in the Highland League scene. He made his Motherwell debut in a 1-2 defeat at Clydebank.

Appearances 78 Goals 0

Jim GARDNER

'Like father like son', was a saying that could apply to the Gardners. Pat had served Motherwell in the 1970s and Jim arrived some twenty years later to continue the family connection. In truth, Jim never quite fulfilled his potential at Motherwell but there were signs that he could pose problems for defences. Eventually his winger skills found a peg at St Mirren in September 1993, where he was part of the deal to bring Paul Lambert to Fir Park, and he later served Stirling Albion.

Appearances 7/8 Goals 0

Pat GARDNER

A forward-running midfielder who joined Motherwell in October 1974

John Gardiner

Pat Gardner

for £12,000, Gardner was signed by Willie McLean from his brother Jim at Dundee United. Pat had been a prolific marksman at Raith before moving to Dunfermline for £17,000 in 1967. At East End Park he thrived, playing in a European Cup Winners Cup semi-final and scoring twice for the Dunfermline side that beat Hearts in the 1968 Scottish Cup final. In 1972 he became Jim McLean's first signing at Dundee United and he helped them to reach the 1974 Scottish Cup final against Celtic, when he netted against Hearts in a replayed semi-final.

His strong running and powerful shooting enticed Motherwell in 1974 and he repaid the club by helping Motherwell squeeze into the inaugural Premier League. However, he lasted just two years at Fir Park before moving on to Arbroath. His son Jim played for

Jim Gardner

Robert Gilchrist

Motherwell briefly in the 1990s. A good, solid performer, he gave the club a much-needed touch of experience at a vital time.

Appearances 29/5 Goals 5

Jim GEDDES

Understudy to Charlie Cox, poor Jim Geddes, who was signed from Forth Wanderers in 1952, enters the Motherwell story under the heading 'one game wonder'. Strictly speaking, he actually played more than one game, though his sole League match came in the 'B' Division campaign of 1953/54, when Motherwell romped to promotion. He did, however, play four League Cup games that season and was in the side that drew 4-4 at St Mirren in a Love Street goal feast in the 1954/55 competition.

Appearances 1 Goals 0

Alec GIBSON

Throughout the war years Alec 'Hoot' Gibson had played and scored frequently for Motherwell. He was on the scoresheet at the start of the 1945/46 season, when Motherwell won 3-0 at Rangers, and clearly was a talented and effective forward. When football proper returned, in the 1946/47 campaign, he found a spot on the right wing but, despite goals against Queen's Park and Falkirk, was soon out of the side, having lost the number 7 jersey to Wilson Humphries.

Appearances 8 Goals 2

Robert GILCHRIST

A robust full-back, Robert made his bow in the spring of 1957 at left-back. Unfortunately, Motherwell lost each of the four games he played that season. With competition from the likes of Pat Holton, Ian MacFadyen and Willie McSeveney, his time at Motherwell was effectively up. He had joined Motherwell from Aldershot, and left at the end of 1957/58.

Appearances 10 Goals 0

Eric GILLESPIE

A Scottish Junior international while with Cambuslang Rangers, Eric tried his luck in England with Burnley before moving to Kilmarnock. It was from Rugby Park that Motherwell signed him in the early 1970s. His handful of Motherwell outings included a Texaco Cup tie against Stoke City. After his spell with Motherwell he played with both Hamilton and Albion Rovers, before being reinstated to the junior ranks with Cumnock.

Appearances 17/1 Goals 0

Jim GILLESPIE

Tall and curly haired, Jim was quite a noticeable figure on the football field. Signed from Standard Wettern, he appeared to have all the attributes required of a centre forward – height, strength and bravery – but the goals just would not come. However, he was at the club in the 1983/84 season, which from an early stage was likely to end in relegation. He enjoyed better times with his next club Morton.

Appearances 12/4 Goals 0

David GOLDIE

Following the loss of Ian St John to Liverpool, Motherwell had the task of seeking a replacement. One such player was David Goldie of Kilsyth Juniors. He made his debut in a 2-1 win over St Mirren and had his first goal under his belt early in the 1962/63 season against Airdrie. But with Bobby Roberts and Joe McBride providing the competition, openings were limited.

Appearances 7 Goals 1

Jim Gillespie

John Goldthorp

John GOLDTHORP

Signed from Lesmahagow Juniors in 1967, Goldthorp was a tall and powerful striker who stayed with Motherwell for eight years. He made his debut against Dunfermline in September 1967 and scored his first goal a week later against Dundee. Manager Bobby Howitt was very pleased with his return but was anxious not to overstrain a troublesome thigh injury that John carried and thus he made just 10 appearances in Motherwell's 1967/68 campaign, which ended in relegation.

Unable to dislodge either McInally or Deans from the centre-spots, it took him longer than expected to become a first team regular, although he had an impact in the promotion winning team of 1969 with 9 goals in the final batch of League matches.

Although Jackie McInally eventually gave way to Goldthorp, the arrival of

Don Goodman

Jim Muir provided new opposition and, although he eventually outstayed Muir, the introduction of Pettigrew and Graham proved the end of his Fir Park career. In 1975 he left to join Morton and he enjoyed considerable success there in Benny Rooney's exciting team. Indeed, he made a remarkable debut, scoring the only goal in the 1976 Renfrewshire Ne'erday derby. John finally had a short spell with Airdrie.

Appearances 142/18 Goals 43

Ian GOODALL

When Wilson Humphries moved infield from the outside-right berth, Goodall occupied the vacant number 7 jersey briefly. He filled it well and laid on a stack of chances for Watson and Mathie, even taking the odd one that fell his way. However, Willie Watters and Willie McCall forced him out and he had to move on. Having been recruited from junior club Kilsyth Rangers in 1948, Ian was released in 1950.

Appearances 16 Goals 2

Don GOODMAN

Arriving at Fir Park in March 1999 with quite a reputation as a goalscorer, Goodman was spotted in his hometown of Leeds. He joined Bradford City as a youngster and was a big hit there. This earned him lucrative moves to West Bromwich Albion, Sunderland and Wolverhampton.

From England he moved to Japan with Hiroshima, before Barnsley took him on loan. When Motherwell stepped in, eyebrows were raised. Here were provincial Motherwell signing a player who had been a £1m buy in previous years and was a well-known figure in the game.

By his own admission it took Don time to settle. In his first season his goal-touch deserted him and he had only one goal when the curtain came down on the season. However, during the millennium campaign he was amongst the goals more frequently and led the line with power and commitment.

Appearances 33/4 Goals 8

John GOODWIN

Signed in 1961 from Carluke Rovers, John was an inside left. He made six outings in the 1962/63 campaign and scored in Motherwell's emphatic 4-1 win at Broomfield. Released in 1964, he reverted to Junior football.

Appearances 8 Goals 1

Sam GOODWIN

A wing-half, Goodwin was a most accomplished performer. He joined

Airdrie in 1965 from Craigmark Burntonians, and thereafter the only problem facing the Diamonds was how to hold on to this talent. Eventually he went south to Crystal Palace in 1971, before Motherwell signed him in 1972. He gave sterling, cultured performances for Motherwell before finally leaving in 1975. It was interesting to note that his time at Airdrie saw him play alongside former Motherwell star Pat Delaney.

Appearances 61/3 Goals 2

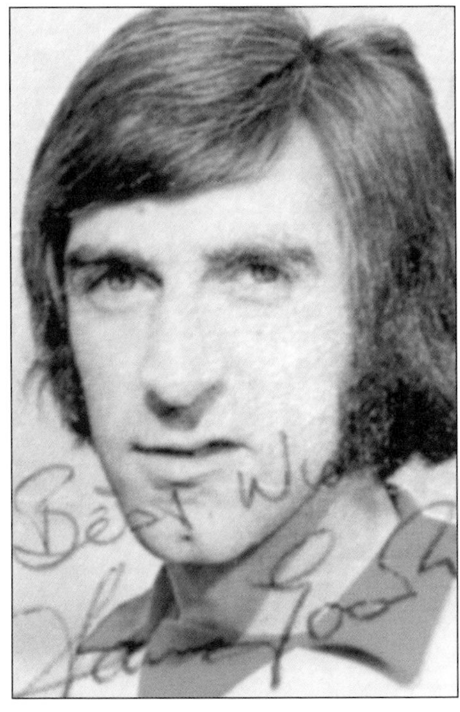

Sam Goodwin

Andy GORAM

Arguably the greatest goalkeeper to represent Scotland in the post-war era, Goram was not particularly big for a 'keeper but a wonderful shot-stopper and the master of the one-on-one situation. Goram was born in Bury, Lancashire with goalkeeping in his genes, as his father Lew had played with Hibernian.

Andy Goram

Andy started his career with Oldham Athletic and made wonderful progress while there, being capped at Under-21 and full international level by Scotland. Hibernian snapped him up for a sizeable fee of £325,000, and he did not disappoint them. Something of a cult hero at Easter Road, he scored from a clearance against Morton, and meanwhile continued his international career.

Rangers bought him for £1 million and he was a key figure in their nine-in-a-row years. Hampered by injury problems, he was eventually freed by Rangers in July 1998. There followed a brief spell in England, during which time he served both Notts County and Sheffield United, before making a lucrative move to Motherwell in January

1999. Although he came with a certain amount of baggage, the club supported him stoutly and he soon regained his finest form. A notable cricketer, having played for Scotland, he became Motherwell captain.

Appearances 35 Goals 0

Archie GOURLAY

When Archie started his senior career with Morton, he blossomed so quickly that many observers suggested that a promising career lay ahead. This seemed assured when he was sold to Newcastle United but, alas, he never made the expected impact on Tyneside and Tommy McLean was able to bring him to Motherwell in March 1992. Again, however, he failed to make the impression expected and he left Motherwell having made a mere 3 outings as a substitute.

Appearances 0/3 Goals 0

Mike GOWER

Signed on loan from Tottenham Hotspur, Gower scored on his debut at Ibrox. However, he was released at the end of the 1998/99 campaign. Aged twenty, he was a former England Schools and Youth cap.

Appearances 8/1 Goals 1

Ally GRAHAM

A 6ft 3in, towering target man, Ally apparently owed his move to Motherwell to a great performance for Ayr United against Rangers in the Scottish Cup, which caught Tommy McLean's eye. Motherwell paid Ayr United £100,000 for him in February 1993 and he made his debut in a 0-4 defeat by Rangers at Fir Park that month. However, he never quite fitted into the scheme of things once inside Fir Park and he was sold to Raith Rovers after only a handful of games. His career continued with Falkirk and Finnish club TPV Tampere, Graham using his tall physique to good effect before he joined Stirling Albion's sizeable clan of ex-Steelmen. Prior to Ayr United he had played with Albion Rovers, Clydebank and Anniesland Waverley.

Appearances 9 Goals 1

Bobby GRAHAM

Motherwell-born, Graham joined Liverpool straight from school and played in Shankly's magnificent side of the 1960s, alongside strikers such as Ian St John and Roger Hunt. His Liverpool debut was spectacular – a hat-trick against Aston Villa. He served the Reds from 1964 through to 1971 and scored 31 goals in 96 appearances before being transferred to Coventry City in March 1972 for £70,000.

As at Liverpool, Ian St John was a colleague and they linked up again at Tranmere when 'The Saint' was coach there. It was therefore little surprise when St John upon his appointment as Motherwell manager looked to Graham to provide guidance up front. It proved to be a very shrewd decision.

He made a quiet debut at Arbroath in September, but finished the season as the club's top scorer. The most dramatic development had been the arrival of Willie Pettigrew, whose raw talent and searing pace were harnessed by Graham's experience and prompting. A delightful partnership was born and Graham enjoyed four seasons of formidable striking at Fir Park.

In the summer of 1977 Bobby moved to Hamilton for £15,000 – a then record fee for Accies.

Appearances 126/6 Goals 37

Bernie GRANT

Season 1983/84 was Motherwell's equivalent of *Ben Hur* with, it seemed, a 'cast of thousands' taking the field. No fewer than thirty-four players featured in that disastrous relegation campaign and few enjoyed the experience. At least Grant, who joined from EK Dynamo, had the satisfaction of saying he made a winning debut, Motherwell recording a 2-1 win at Easter Road when he made his bow.

Appearances 5/1 Goals 0

John GRAY

A product of Eastercraig Youth Club, John was rated the discovery of the 1972/73 season. An artistic ball-player, he proved a tricky right-winger and made 13 League outings that very season. He did not realise his early potential, however, and was released in 1974.

Appearances 22/3 Goals 2

John Gray

Bobby Graham

Jim GRIFFIN

Signed from Fir Park Boys Club in June 1985, Jim's career was cut short by injury after making steady progress in the first team. He was granted a testimonial against Wolves and thereafter joined the backroom staff at Fir Park, a position he held until 1999.

Initially a part-time footballer, he served his apprenticeship as an engineer and had an HNC in multi-disciplinary engineering. He made his first team debut in a 0-4 defeat by Hibernian in 1986 and, in truth, made rather slow progress for the first five years of his Fir Park career. Much of that, however, was due to injuries, the most notable of which were inflicted by team-mate Colin McNair in a training ground assault.

By the early 1990s, Jim was beginning

Jim Griffin

to make strides in the first team and bagging a few goals. It was therefore no surprise when he played a key role in the 1991 Scottish Cup-winning team, providing the cross from which Iain Ferguson headed the opening goal.

His loss through injury was a blow but his steady accumulation of coaching certificates showed he had always thought ahead. He became Motherwell's caretaker-manager in February 1998 and when Harri Kampman took over, Jim became head coach.

Appearances 92 Goals 6

James GROZIER
An inside forward, James was signed from Glenafton in 1950. A small man, he was nevertheless a clever little player whose only misfortune was to arrive at Motherwell during a spell when they had an exceptional surplus of inside men. Ultimately, the presence of Jim Forrest and Wilson Humphries restricted him to just a handful of matches and he was released in 1953.

Appearances 3 Goals 1

H

Stephen HALLIDAY
Signed by Harri Kampman in July 1998, Stephen was a native of Sunderland and had played with Hartlepool before moving to Fir Park. He flitted in and out of the team early in the 1998/99 season but eventually made only four League outings that season. He did score a League Cup winner at East Fife that season and his stocky build and no nonsense approach were clearly what had caught Motherwell's eye.

Appearances 5(4) Goals 0

Dick HAMILTON
In five years at Motherwell, Dick (or 'Richard' to give him his full Christian name) was more often than not the reserve 'keeper. When called upon he performed admirably but John Johnston was a hard man to shift from between the sticks. Depressed by the lack of openings, Dick was granted a free transfer in 1952. It is difficult to avoid the feeling that he was extremely

Scott HOWIE

In October 1994 Alex McLeish signed Scott for £200,000 from Norwich City. A Scotland Under-21 international, he had started his career with Clyde and a number of Scottish clubs were disappointed when he swapped the Bully Wee for East Anglia. At Fir Park he vied with Stevie Woods for the number 1 jersey and made just under 100 appearances in all competitions before moving on to Reading. He was capped 5 times by Scotland at Under-21 level.

Appearances 69 Goals 0

Bert HOWIESON

Bert had a high profile start to his career, joining Leeds United as a youngster. However, he never quite broke through at Elland Road and he moved to Dundee United in November 1960. In four seasons at Tannadice he scored 6 times in 67 matches, but was in and out of the first team and so elected to join Motherwell in 1965. The move did not quite work out and he played just 3 League games, without scoring.

Appearances 3 Goals 0

Scott Howie

Ronnie HUME

Five games in April 1964, back to back, constituted Ronnie Hume's career at Fir Park after he was signed from Partick Thistle. The season was fizzling out to a dull end and Ronnie did not hang about in the close season, opting instead to move to South Africa and Highland Park in 1965.

Appearances 5 Goals 0

Wilson HUMPHRIES

Born in Motherwell in 1928, Wilson joined the club as a seventeen-year-old. Well-built and powerful, he was to make 199 League appearances for Motherwell in the ten seasons immediately after the war. Like many in his era, he would have had more appearances but for National Service. Always a likely goalscorer, he ended up with a most impressive haul of 69 strikes.

Picking highlights from his Motherwell career is not an easy task. He scored six goals in the record 12-1 win over Dundee United in 1954 and scored vital cup goals in Motherwell's successful 1952 campaign. Indeed, he chipped in with 5 goals as Motherwell finally broke their Scottish Cup jinx. In the League Cup he was prolific too, netting 31 goals in just 47 ties. He was capped by both the Scottish League and Scotland before he moved to St Mirren in May 1956.

He spent a season with the Paisley club before moving to Dundee United and then Hamilton Accies, finally retiring

Wilson Humphries

as a player in 1962. He then enjoyed a coaching career that included stints with St Mirren, Motherwell, Hibernian and Airdrie. His involvement in football carried him through to 1982.

On reflection, it was strange that he should have enjoyed such a prolonged football career, for he was a well-qualified man to pursue such a precarious occupation. Having graduated from Glasgow University with a BA, he entered teaching and taught several future Motherwell players at Dalziel High.

Appearances 199 Goals 69

Ally HUNTER

One of the best goalkeepers of his era, Ally was a star with Kilmarnock and Celtic long before he came to Motherwell. Sadly, his career was on the wane by the time he arrived at Fir Park from Celtic for £40,000 in April 1976 and he made only 8 outings for Motherwell before being moved on to St Mirren in October 1977. Ally won several Scotland caps and a Scottish League Cup winners badge, in a career that effectively began in the Junior ranks with Johnstone Burgh before he moved to Kilmarnock in 1970. Kilmarnock had six years' good service before transferring Ally to Celtic for £40,000 in 1973.

Appearances 8 Goals 0

Jackie HUNTER

Whole-hearted and rumbustious, Jackie was well liked by the Fir Park faithful. Born in Leith, he joined The Steelmen in 1948 from Tranent Juniors. He had difficulty breaking into the first eleven but served notice of his intention most graphically in the 1950/51 season, bagging 14 reserve team goals.

His big break came when the club found themselves in the 'B' Division. He and Wilson Humphries were rampant in the 'B' fixture against Dundee United, which Motherwell ultimately won 12-1, Jackie scoring four and Wilson six. The week after his foursome against United he scored a hat-trick against Morton and he ended the season with 28 goals from 26 games, a truly excellent statistic.

Jackie spent ten seasons with Motherwell and was frequently amongst the goals. His Motherwell highlights would surely include his appearance as outside-right when Motherwell were beaten 2-4 by Hearts in the 1954/55 League Cup final. He joined Dundee United in 1958, seemingly forgiven for, or perhaps remembered for, the 12-1 match!

Appearances 89 Goals 55

Robert HUNTER

A native of Shotts, Bobby had scored 34 times for Hamilton in the 1950/51 season when Motherwell signed him in the summer of 1951. The surprise, therefore, was that he then found himself restricted to just 2 League games in six years, and it mattered little that he scored in one of those matches. He was very popular at Fir Park but could not produce the form many were certain he was capable of. Ultimately he played most of his football while a Motherwell player during his National Service in England. That experience with Swindon Town was the forerunner to a permanent move to non-League Poole after he was freed by Motherwell. Bobby had been a noted tennis player and won a few local titles in Lanarkshire.

Jackie Hunter

Willie Hunter

Appearances 2 Goals 1

Willie HUNTER

Bobby Ancell signed Willie from Edinburgh Norton in the summer of 1957. Within months it was clear that the manager had snapped up a dazzling footballer who was both a brilliant ball player and a determined performer. Ancell would later say that Hunter was the most skilled of the 'Ancell Babes', a wonderful compliment considering that Andy Weir and Pat Quinn were also in that team.

Always amongst the goals for Motherwell, Hunter laid on far more than he scored, a proud claim given that he bagged over 50 competitive goals. He won 3 caps for Scotland whilst at Motherwell. The only black spot in his Fir Park career was a troublesome string of injuries. He finally left Fir Park in 1967 and had spells with Detroit Cougars and Hibernian. Given that he had been raised in the Abbeyhill district of Edinburgh and was a life-long Hibee, that proved a source of great satisfaction to him. He had spells in coaching and management when his playing days ended, most notably at Queen of the South and Inverness Caledonian. Outside football, he revealed himself to be as comfortable with the pen as the football and was author of several books.

Appearances 229 Goals 40

I

Willie IRVINE

Willie began his senior career with Celtic, signing for Jock Stein's club in 1973 as a sixteen-year-old. He was farmed out to Whitburn Juniors before being called up to Celtic Park. Competition was inevitably keen at Parkhead and he

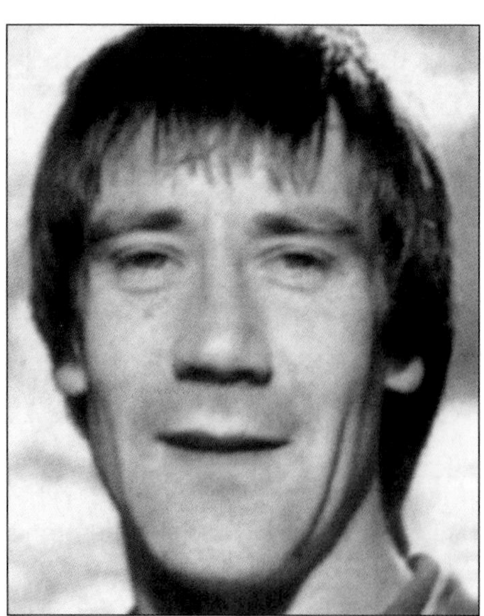

Willie Irvine

was freed in 1977, having failed to reach the first team. He then went from junior football to Alloa Athletic, bagged 29 goals in a season and in 1979 Motherwell snapped him up for £25,000. Given that he had already netted 13 goals for Alloa that term, there were understandably high hopes for him. Scoring on his debut against Dundee United, he quickly revealed himself to be a competent poacher with great pace.

In the promotion winning team of 1981/82 he was Motherwell's top scorer, with 21 goals. However, like manager Davie Hay, he was to leave in the shadow of that triumph, electing to move to Hibernian. While at Hibs he was the second top scorer in the Premier League during the 1983/84 campaign. Willie was nicknamed 'Noddy' by virtue of his unusual running style, and if he had a fault it was perhaps that he was exceedingly left-sided.

Appearances 118/3 Goals 49

J. IRVING

Standing in for Brown at centre forward early on in the 1946/47 season, Irving played against both Hearts and Queen's Park, but scored in neither game and soon drifted from the Fir Park scene.

Appearances 2 Goals 0

J

Gunni JONSSON

An Icelandic central defender brought to Fir Park on trial by Alex McLeish, Johnson played in two Premier League games

against Aberdeen and St Johnstone in the autumn of 1997 but was not signed on a permanent basis.
Appearances 2 Goals 0

Joe JOHNSTON
A local lad, Joe graduated from BB football and came to Fir Park from Renfrew Juniors in 1937. An outside-left, he played many fine games for Motherwell and in the latter stages of his career featured strongly as a left-half. A grand player and a loyal clubman, Joe joined Albion Rovers as a player coach at the end of the 1951/52 season.

His career has the classic profile of the player who was robbed of continuity by the war. Johnston was in the army and thus had few opportunities to represent his club. When he came back in peacetime he was challenged by Barclay and Aitkenhead and never really established himself.

Yet, for all the disruptions his career endured, he did carve a niche for himself in the annals of Motherwell history. In the season of 1941/42 he scored a hat-trick in a sensational 6-2 victory over Hearts at Tynecastle, and he had a hat-trick in Motherwell's 3-2 win at Cappielow against Morton in October 1947. His first goal had come in an equally exciting game, a 3-5 defeat at Third Lanark on 11 December 1937.

The curtain came down on Joe's career on 6 October 1951, in a 4-0 home win over Queen of the South. Such a farewell was a fitting finale for a loyal servant who, despite his broken service, was with Motherwell for fourteen seasons.
Appearances 79 Goals 20

John JOHNSTON
Born in Bo'ness, John joined the Motherwell in 1941 from Armadale Thistle, having earlier starred with his local Academy and Winchburgh Albion. Indeed, he was a provisional Rangers signing when only sixteen and managed a few reserve outings for the 'Gers, but was never called up to serve in the first eleven.

John Johnston

Johnston was a stalwart Motherwell 'keeper of the mid-1940s and early '50s, who frequently had his name incorrectly spelled with an 'e' at the end. Agile, brave and a wonderful shot-stopper, he was highly respected in the Scottish game and his only notable absence came in the early 1950s when he was injured and lost his place to the admirable Dick Hamilton. Indeed from October 1943 through to September 1949 he did not miss a single Motherwell League match and totted up no fewer than

Alex Jones

180 consecutive League appearances. That run came to an end after the first match of the 1949/50 season against Falkirk, but John was back for the last game of the same season; unfortunately it was no glory return and he could not prevent East Fife winning 4-3 at Fir Park. By coincidence, his last ever Motherwell game was also against East Fife and again ended in defeat – this time by 3 goals to 2 – and throughout his career he found the Fifers a difficult club to keep at bay.

John was a member of the Summer Cup winning side in 1944, a memorable occasion as it saw Motherwell smash their long-standing Hampden cup final jinx. Johnston was to win other medals and enjoy further Hampden occasions. In 1950 he picked up a League Cup winner's medal against Hibernian, after unlucky Dick Hamilton had been ruled out of the final because of injury after playing in every previous match. The League Cup, if one includes the Southern League Cup, was to be a favourite competition for Johnston who played in a quite remarkable 71 League Cup ties.

There were also two Scottish Cup final appearances for Johnston. In 1951 he was in the side beaten by Celtic, but the following year he played in all 10 matches as Motherwell marched to their Hampden triumph over Dundee. He finally left the club in 1955, as the much younger Hastie Weir, recruited from Queen's Park, established himself.

On one notable occasion John saved two penalties against Hibernian at Easter Road. The match took place in 1949 but the duo of stops mattered little, as Hibs already held a 5-1 lead but the match finished with that score-line because of his heroics. His was a long and interesting career and perhaps suffered less than most from the impact of the war. John died in Law Hospital on 21 January 1989, just one day after the death of former team-mate Willie Redpath.

Appearances 323 Goals 0

Alex JONES

A towering centre half, Alex was signed by Tommy McLean from Rochdale in January 1992 for £35,000. Given his height and grit, he always looked capable of doing the job. However, he was not the most mobile of central defenders and found some of the nippy Scottish strikers a real handful. He had played in England for several years

before joining Motherwell and amongst his former employers were Oldham, Stockport, Preston and Carlisle United. He went back to Rochdale after his stint at Motherwell, then played with Halifax, Stalybridge Celtic, Chorley, Southport and Lancaster City.
Appearances 12 Goals 1

Sandy JONES
In the early 1960s Motherwell experimented with a string of centre forwards, few of whom fitted the bill. One such was Sandy who had a single outing before being moved on to Ayr United. Signed as a nineteen-year-old from Coltness, he played his only 90 minutes in a 2-1 win over St Mirren in March 1962. He did, however, play in the Friendship Trophy against Nîmes Olympique and scored Motherwell's goal in the 1-2 defeat at Fir Park. It was in 1962 that he joined Ayr United.
Appearances 1 Goals 0

Joe JOYCE
A huge bearded man, Joe came to Motherwell in the Ian St John management era, and first impressions suggested here was a figure who could dominated the heart of the defence. Indeed during the 1973/74 season he and Willie Pettigrew were earmarked as the two reserves most likely to break through into the first team. Joe was tried in several positions in the reserves and a first team career looked likely. However, appearances proved deceptive and Joe did not impress sufficiently, despite his Liverpool heritage. He soon left the club, having made two brief cameo outings as a substitute in the 1974/75 campaign.
Appearances 0/2 Goals 0

K

Tony KANE
A midfielder, Tony joined Motherwell in 1978 from Lanark United. Despite remaining at Fir Park for a couple of seasons, he was unable to establish himself in the first team for any length of time and his outings were confined to the 1979/80 First Division term.
Appearances 11/7 Goals 0

Mikko KAVEN
Understudy goalkeeper in the Finnish national side, Kaven was signed by Motherwell's Finnish manager Harri Kampman. Costing £50,000 from HJK

Mikko Kaven

Archie Kelly

Helsinki, he did not last very long at Motherwell, leaving during 1998/99.
Appearances 16 Goals 0

Archie KELLY
Born in Paisley on 9 December 1921, Archie was a star junior player with Arthurlie before turning senior with Hearts in 1943. He was a huge success at Tynecastle, netting over a hundred goals in just over four years. He once scored seven goals against Albion Rovers, when in direct opposition to Jock Stein, and broke a goal post (and his collar-bone) against Kilmarnock when he collided with it! Indeed, Archie was a hard physical player but one with a skilful touch in front of goal, and that tempted Aberdeen in 1947.

That December he went to Pittodrie in exchange for George Hamilton, with a £7,000 cash adjustment in Aberdeen's favour. His first goal for the Dons came against Motherwell, but it was while he was with Motherwell that he really shone. He joined up on 5 November 1949 and the fireworks started thereafter; indeed, he scored on his debut against Clyde.

What was the highlight of his Fir Park career? It could be the goal in the Scottish Cup final win over Dundee, or the first goal in the 3-0 win over Hibs in the League Cup final. However, a case could be made for his extraordinary success against the Old Firm, whom he always gave a hard time, netting twice in a 4-0 hammering of Rangers. He also played in the 5-5 Scottish Cup draw at Aberdeen (Motherwell lost the replay 1-6!). Mention of Aberdeen brings to mind his foursome against them in March 1950 at Fir Park.

In October 1953 Archie moved to Stirling Albion for £2,600 and from there he went to Ayr United in January 1955. He was not retained at the end of the season and therein lies an interesting story. He relates how he was signed specifically to help the club enjoy a good Scottish Cup run. United drew 1-1 at Inverness Caley and slumped to a shock 2-4 home defeat in the replay. For a man who had scored in the 1952 Cup Final it was a bitter blow, but the management at Ayr were even more disappointed and released Archie at the end of the League campaign. Nevertheless, his 11 League games for the Honest Men had brought 7 goals. This was not the end of his playing career and he started the next season starring at Cowdenbeath.

Archie was undoubtedly one of the genuine heroes of Motherwell supporters; he chased every cause, always gave 100 per cent and, as a goalscorer, created excitement. Had he played today he would have proved extremely popular with both press and fans.

Appearances 104 Goals 66

Ben KEMBLE

Kemble was signed by Billy Davies just hours after Motherwell had lost famously 5-6 at home in the SPL to Aberdeen on 25 October 1999. Having been with NAC Nijmegan and EVC Eindhoven (not to be confused with PSV), he made his bow against Dundee United in a 2-0 win at Tannadice and was seen as something of a lucky mascot. Raised in Surinam, he played with a club called Robin Hood and went on to play 30 times for his country. He was actually spotted by Motherwell while playing a trial for Tranmere Rovers.

Appearances 25 Goals 1

Ben Kemble

Alex Kennedy

Alex KENNEDY

Red-headed Alex was tall, athletic and possessed a good footballing brain. He came to Motherwell in 1982 from the hot-bed of Ayrshire Junior football, Craigmark Burntonians, and certainly knew how to handle the physical side of the game. He went to Partick Thistle for £30,000 in 1989, Motherwell having used him in both defence and midfield.

Appearances 43/7 Goals 6

Ian KENNEDY

A busy player, Ian starred in the team of Willie Pettigrew and Bobby Graham in the 1970s, and although essentially he played just a cameo role, he was a useful player. Always full of endeavour, he was a good 'team player' and created openings for those around him. On reflection his career should have offered

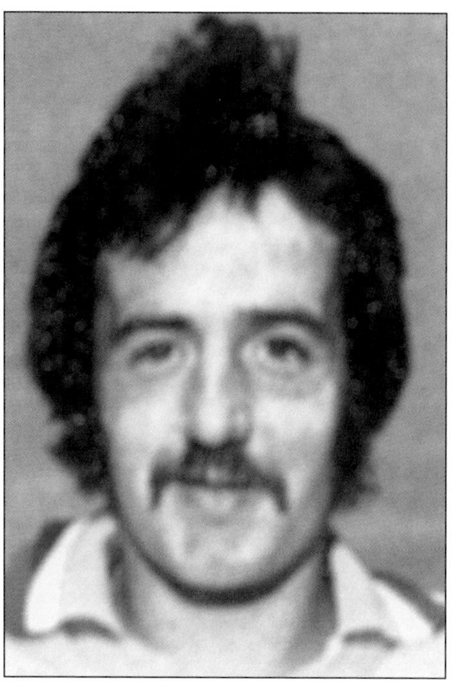

Ian Kennedy

more than it did and by the time he left Motherwell the fire in his game seemed to have been extinguished.

Appearances 45/19 Goals 2

Archie KERR

Recruited from Camelon Juniors in 1953, Archie was a tricky outside right who never quite managed to establish himself as a first team regular. During his National Service he played with Shrewsbury Town, but even on returning to Motherwell he was not able to make the winger's berth his own. A clever player, he joined Gerry Baker at St Mirren in 1960.

Appearances 31 Goals 6

Jerry KERR

In the first two seasons after the war Andy Paton missed only two matches in each. Thus for four games Kerr, on loan from Edinburgh-based side St Bernards, stood in. Given that one of those matches was a 2-1 win over an up and coming Hibernian side, he could be well pleased with his roll as deputy.

After he left Motherwell he eventually became manager of Dundee United. He is credited with starting the lucrative 'Taypools', which allowed the financing of the 'Viking Invasion', and also established United financially. He was followed in the manager's office by Jim McLean, whose younger brother Tommy would later manage Motherwell.

Appearances 4 Goals 0

Archie Kerr

Albert KIDD

One game stands out in the career of Albert Kidd, and he was not in a Motherwell shirt! While playing for Dundee, Albert scored twice against Hearts on the final day of the 1985/86 League campaign. The defeat cost

Hearts the League championship and earned Kidd headlines throughout Scotland.

--Signed along with Joe Carson in December 1979 from Arbroath, Albert had previously been with Brechin City and proved a useful addition to the Motherwell squad, being adept in front of goal. However, he was not happy in Lanarkshire and accepted a move to Dundee in 1981 as their record signing at £80,000 with little hesitation. The rest, as they say, is history.

Appearances 53 Goals 18

Willie KILMARNOCK

A native of Irvine, Willie went from Boys' Brigade football to Irvine Meadow and then on to Renfrew Juniors. He joined Motherwell at the beginning of the 1939/40 season, when Motherwell

Albert Kidd

Willie Kilmarnock

greats of the 1930s such as Ben Ellis, Hugh Wales, Tommy McKenzie, John Blair, Duncan Ogilvie, Hutton Bremner and George Stevenson were still on the playing staff. By the time he left he was without doubt of that calibre himself.

Willie was to prove a great club man and notable captain, remaining at Fir Park until 1956/57, when he was transferred to Airdrieonians. That he played over 100 League Cup ties demonstrates his longevity. His loyal service saw him collect Scottish Cup winner's and loser's medals, League Cup winner's and loser's medals, a 'B' Division championship badge, a war-time international cap (1944) against England at Wembley and a League international cap against the League of Ireland in 1948/49. These achievements make him an automatic choice for the Motherwell hall of fame.

Just as the Stevenson and Ferrier left-wing partnership became renowned in the 1930s, the Willie Kilmarnock and Archie Shaw full-back pairing was famous in the 1940s and '50s. So much so that on 1 January 1957, before the derby match with Airdrie at Fir Park, both Willie and Archie received rose bowls and fountain pens from the Motherwell Supporters' Club as recognition of their long partnership. On that day Willie captained Airdrie and Motherwell won 2-0.

In his day he was recognised as one of the strongest dead-ball kickers in Scotland. The goal he scored in the 2-1 victory over East Fife in the semi-final of the League Cup in 1954/55 was ample evidence of this. A couple of years earlier he made an even more desperate scoring contribution, netting on the penultimate and final Saturdays of the season as Motherwell battled against relegation in 1953. He was very fast for a full-back and was never really beaten by an opposing winger because of his speed of recovery. In match programmes other clubs frequently described him as a 'wholehearted defender who goes to the ball and clears with decision'.

A Scottish schoolboy international while attending Irvine Academy, Kilmarnock was to be linked with Alan Craig in a quite extraordinary coincidence. In the 1954 Scottish Cup semi-final draw with Celtic at Hampden he scored an own goal which was described as being headed with the same velocity, at the same height and into the same goal as the Alan Craig header in the 1931 Scottish Cup Final, against the same opposition in a match which also finished 2-2!

While Willie achieved much in his long career with Motherwell, his finest memory will always be that of bringing the Scottish Cup back to Fir Park after the splendid victory over Dundee in 1952. No other Motherwell player had previously achieved this and as one of the best captains in the history of the club, perhaps it was fitting that Willie Kilmarnock should have that honour.

Appearances 452 Goals 26

Paul KINNAIRD

Arguably the nomad of Scottish football, Paul played for so many clubs that it is hardly surprising that he managed to fit in a spell with Motherwell, especially as Tommy McLean, forever a dabbler in the market, was Fir Park supremo at the time!

Undoubtedly a talented winger,

Paul Kinnaird

Paul's weakness was probably his inconsistency. He joined Motherwell from Dundee United and went on to play over 30 games without scoring a goal. How ironic that Motherwell should sell him to St Mirren and then watch in horror as he ended his drought with the only goal of a League Cup tie – against Motherwell!

After St Mirren he tried various clubs and in 1999 was with Ross County in the Scottish Second Division. His full list of clubs reads as follows: Norwich City, Dundee United, Motherwell, St Mirren, Partick Thistle, Shrewsbury Town (on loan), St Johnstone, Dunfermline Athletic, Derry City, Scarborough, Ayr United, Stranraer and Ross County. Paul also had a short spell in Iceland between his stints at Ayr United and Stranraer.

He joined Motherwell in 1988 from Dundee United for £20,000 and was sold for a healthy profit at £90,000 to St Mirren in 1989.

Appearances 34 Goals 0

Stevie KIRK

Ostensibly a midfielder, Kirk was a free-scoring player who carved a niche for himself in the Motherwell sides of the late 1980s and early 1990s. He not only scored the goal that won the 1991 Scottish Cup final but contributed several valuable counters en route to Hampden, all of them from the substitutes' bench.

An enigmatic performer, he was a more than capable goalkeeper as he proved in matches at both Hearts and Dundee, when he stood in after departures and dismissals. All in all, Kirk was a character capable of exciting and depressing the Motherwell supporters with remarkable frequency.

His career began as a youngster with Buckhaven Hibs, from whence he moved to East Fife. As a seventeen-year-old he spent the 1979/80 League campaign with the Fifers in the Second Division and scored twice in 25 League appearances. He played the following two seasons in England with Stoke City but made only 12 outings for the Potteries side. Nevertheless, his experience of competitive English football was to stand him in good stead as his career progressed.

Stevie Kirk

In 1982 he returned to Scotland with Partick Thistle but he never made a competitive outing for the Jags and he rejoined East Fife. He finished the 1982/83 season having scored 8 goals in 25 matches for the Bayview side and never looked back. By the summer of 1985, East Fife were destined for better things and Kirk was selected for the Scottish pool competing in the Four Nations Tournament.

After narrowly failing to gain

promotion with East Fife in 1986 he was sold to Motherwell for a bargain £35,000, with Ray Blair moving from Fir Park to Fife as a make-weight. He had finished as top scorer at East Fife, with 14 League goals, and this form did not desert him in the Premier League with Motherwell.

He made his Motherwell debut against Hibs on 23 August 1986 and a few days later scored twice against Hamilton Accies at Douglas Park. His contribution in his debut season was immense and he scored 10 goals; a figure only centre forward Andy Walker could match.

In 1989 Motherwell narrowly avoided relegation and Stevie's quartet of goals in the 4-0 win over St Mirren late in the season were a key factor in staying up. In all competitions he amassed 18 goals, despite always fulfilling the role of midfield schemer, but orthodox he never was and his ability to get into scoring positions was quite remarkable.

The Cup-winning season in 1991 was an astonishing adventure for Kirk. He came off the bench to score the only goal in a shock win against holders Aberdeen at Pittodrie and thereafter netted against Falkirk, Morton – in a penalty shoot-out – and Celtic before popping in an extra-time winner against Dundee United in the final itself. All this in a season in which he suffered a fractured cheekbone and missed six weeks!

As the 1990s progressed, Kirk continued to prove his enormous worth as a goalscoring midfielder, going on to surpass Willie Pettigrew as Motherwell's all-time top Premier Division goalscorer. He took his coaching certificates while at Motherwell and when he finished his playing career, after spells at Falkirk and Raith Rovers, he briefly went into management, with East Fife.

Appearances 301 Goals 63

Miodrag KRIVOKAPIC

Having served his early career in his native Yugoslavia with the mighty Red Star Belgrade, it was clear that 'Mio' was a player of some considerable quality. He proved this when joining Jim McLean's Dundee United in 1988. Cool and experienced, he was a great success at United, playing in the Scottish Cup final against Motherwell. Unfortunately, he fell out with McLean and was sidelined for several months in a messy contractual dispute.

However, when Tommy McLean signed 'Mio' for Motherwell, the player continued his good form. His only goal was memorable, coming as it did after a lung-bursting run upfield at Easter Road and being followed by prolonged celebrations with the Motherwell support behind that goal. He returned to Motherwell in 1999 in a coaching capacity, having carried out similar duties for Hamilton Accies.

Appearances 71 Goals 1

Elroy KROMHEER

Tommy McLean had a knack of dabbling in the transfer market and coming up with real surprises and Elroy was one of them. A tall, Dutch central defender, he looked useful when he played but his outings were seriously curtailed by injury. He left the club having failed to make either of the central defensive positions his own. Clearly others must have seen the potential too and he

Miodrag Krivokapic

popped up at Reading during Tommy Burns' reign as manager there. Burns, having earlier managed Celtic, would undoubtedly have been amongst his admirers. Elroy had cost Motherwell £150,000 when joining in July 1992

Elroy Kromheer

from FC Volendaam.
Appearances 11/1 Goals 0

L

Paul LAMBERT
A super midfielder, Paul was outstanding for St Mirren as a youngster. He won 11 Scotland Under-21 caps while at Paisley and had captained the Scotland Under-18 side. When Motherwell captured his signature in September 1993 for £125,000, it heralded the beginning of a few years in which Motherwell had a wonderful midfield. Paul was elegant, economical and a wonderful team player. Never too flashy, he was a great worker and a most supportive colleague.

He left under the Bosman Ruling in the summer of 1996 and the move caused considerable pain to Motherwell, for at the time he was surely worth in excess of £1million. Alas, Dortmund were able to prise him away for nothing and during his spell in Germany he won a European Cup medal with them – the first British player to do so with a foreign club. He did return to Scotland, but in the colours of Celtic, and Motherwell were given a fine example of what they were missing when he scored a wonderful goal for Celtic at Fir Park on 3 October 1998 as Motherwell went down 1-2. A Scotland international, Lambert was surely one of the best midfielders to serve Motherwell in the modern era.
Appearances 103 Goals 6

Mike LARNACH
Mike was a prolific goalscorer at Clydebank, and 62 goals in 160 outings made him highly attractive. It was Newcastle United who captured his signature, but he was unable to set the heather on fire for the Magpies and joined Motherwell in the late 1970s.

Hailing from Lybster, Caithness, he cost Motherwell £75,000 in 1978 and made his debut in August of that year against Partick Thistle. He never quite displayed the goalscoring form at Motherwell that had marked his Clydebank career and he had the misfortune to be in the Motherwell side humbled 0-8 at Pittodrie against Aberdeen.

In September 1980 he joined Ayr United for £30,000, following former Motherwell team-mates Jimmy Lindsay

Paul Lambert

and Stuart Rennie to Somerset Park. Freed by Ayr in 1983, he later served both Stenhousemuir and Clydebank. His early career had seen him capped

Mike Larnach

by Scotland at youth level while with Campsie Black Watch Juveniles, before going to Kilbowie Park.

Appearances 49/9 Goals 7

Dave LATCHFORD

A member of the famous footballing family (one brother, Bob, was an England centre forward and another, Peter, a Celtic goalkeeper) Dave never quite lived up to expectations at Fir Park. He kept goal for Motherwell at the start of the 1978/79 season and the club lost seven out of the eight games in which he played, conceding 19 goals in the process. Staying but a few months, his performances were without any great distinction and he was replaced by Stuart Rennie. A sizeable lad, he had joined Birmingham City when he was only eighteen and represented England Youths. Powerfully built, he tipped the scales at fourteen and half stones and lent his considerable frame to the Barnsley cause from March 1979.

Appearances 8 Goals 0

Kirkie LAWSON

A bubbly striker who scored 14 League goals for Motherwell in 65 matches. He came to the club from Blantrye Vics, where he won a Scottish Junior Cup medal in 1970 and was capable of some nice touches and strong finishing. He left in 1973 for Falkirk when it was clear that Goldthorp and Graham were the preferred front two. After some memorable goals for the Bairns he returned to Lanarkshire when joining Hamilton Accies in 1976, and scored 6 goals in 26 games there before returning to the junior ranks with Shettleston.

Appearances 57/8 Goals 14

Joni LEHTONEN

A Finnish midfielder, Joni was signed by Alex McLeish in late 1996. Aged

Dave Latchford

Kirkie Lawson

twenty-three, he made his debut from the bench in a 4-2 win at Kilmarnock in which Tommy Coyne scored a hat-trick and John Philliben grabbed a rare goal. His previous club had been FC Ilves but he found the jump from the amateur set-up in Finland to the Scottish professional League just a little too much.
Appearances 4/2 Goals 0

William LEISHMAN
This player had a couple of games at right-back in the 1973/74 season and made a further appearance in the opening game of the 1974/75 season, against Dundee United. This constituted the total League career of Bill Leishman.
Appearances 3 Goals 0

William LEITCH
How many players in their time at Motherwell have scored as many goals as they have played games? Not many, and thus William Leitch falls into a special category. In 1946/47 he scored against Queen's Park, Hamilton, Queen of the South and Clyde. His only blank came against St Mirren. Signed from Wishaw High School, he was released in 1949.
Appearances 5 Goals 5

Mark LEONARD
Mark came to Motherwell on loan from St Mirren, with a view to a permanent transfer. However, the deal was never done and Mark went back to Paisley to rejoin the Buddies. He played in ten matches, four of them as a sub, but Motherwell ended the 1978/79 season hopelessly relegated and it was not a good time to be at Fir Park.
Appearances 6/4 Goals 0

Stefan LINDQVIST
Perhaps impressed by the success of Larsson (Celtic) and Oloffson (Dundee United), Harri Kampman recruited fellow Scandinavian Lindqvist. Although thirty years old, he had much to commend him to the club. Capped 5 times by Sweden, Lindqvist had played with clubs such as Neuchatel Xamax in Switzerland and Halmstad in Sweden and had experience of the Champions League. He looked the part at Motherwell, lending authority to the Fir Park midfield. Tall and strong, he could hold the ball, fend off challenges and bring those around him into the game; in short he was a midfield general. Alas, he played only until the end of the 1997/98 campaign before moving on. His only goal for the club came in a 1-1 draw with Kilmarnock.
Appearances 5/1 Goals 1

George Lindsay

Jim LINDSAY

Signed in 1976 from Fir Park Boys' Club, much was expected of this sprightly winger. However, Jim never lived up to the expectations and moved to Ayr United in 1979 as part of a complex deal that saw Stuart Rennie, Jim Lindsay and £75,000 head to Somerset in exchange for Hugh Sproat. Jim made his debut for Motherwell in the Premier League in April 1977, when Motherwell somehow played eight League games in the month. His first goal for the club was a penalty in a 2-1 win over Morton at Cappielow.

Appearances 11/10 Goals 1

Graham LLOYD

Born in January 1951, goalkeeper Graham was a former Liverpool apprentice and came to Motherwell in

Jim Lindsay

George LINDSAY

A speedy winger, George played with Carluke Juniors for just six months before moving to Motherwell. He enjoyed a quite spectacular debut scoring in a League match on 15 October 1960 against Third Lanark, although his efforts could not prevent a remarkable 4-5 defeat. Given that he had trained at Fir Park while a schoolboy at Wishaw High School, his arrival had been no real surprise.

He made just 18 outings that season and it was not until the 1962/63 campaign that he secured a regular spot. His pace and trickery marked him out as a match winner and he frequently sent an anticipatory 'buzz' around Fir Park. He was given a free transfer in 1968.

Appearances 159 Goals 27

the wake of the Ian St John-revolution. Signed in 1974, he played in just nine games before being freed. In reality Graham served his time at Motherwell as a back-up to the very capable Stuart Rennie. There were nine matches for Lloyd in the 1974/75 season, but no cup games, and given that Motherwell marched to the Scottish Cup semi-finals it was clear whom manager Willie McLean regarded as his first choice. Lloyd followed St John to Portsmouth and made 73 outings for Pompey between 1975 and 1976.

Appearances 9 Goals 0

James LONIE

Played one, scored one – not a bad record for a forward. The game in question was the final League match of the 1962/63 season and Motherwell defeated Raith Rovers 5-1. Away from League football he had scored in a League Cup game against Falkirk at Brockville. James was signed in 1962 from Grangemouth United and was released in 1964.

Appearances 1 Goals 1

Bert LOGAN

Signed in 1965 from junior side Tranent, Bert was a wing-half who made just one appearance for Motherwell, in a 3-0 home win over Falkirk in February 1966.

Appearances 1 Goals 0

Kenny LYALL

Kenny arrived at Motherwell in December 1983 from Rangers. He came together with Kenny Black, both youngsters being accepted in exchange for goalkeeper Nicky Walker, who made the reverse trip to Ibrox. A left-footed midfielder, Lyall had made

Kenny Lyall

a dozen outings for Rangers and he barely bettered that total at Motherwell, where he failed to impose himself on the scheme of things. He moved to St Johnstone in a deal that brought Raymond Blair to Fir Park. Lyall later played for Brechin City.

Appearances 18/1 Goals 2

Colin McADAM

Brother of Tom, Colin joined Motherwell from Dumbarton for £30,000 in 1975 and was a great signing. Alas, he was, like his brother, able to play at both centre forward and centre half and

Colin McAdam

Tom McAdam

Motherwell never seemed to know which was better. Ultimately he fell between two stools and his record of 3 goals in over 50 games was scant reward, especially when compared to what he later achieved with Partick Thistle, whom he joined for £25,000 in March 1978. From Maryhill he moved on to Rangers and Hearts. The impression given is one of a player who was not properly used by the club.

Appearances 48/14 Goals 3

Tom McADAM

At the age of sixteen Tom joined Dumbarton and he spent five years there before moving to Dundee United. Always capable of playing in defence and attack, he was snapped up by Celtic in 1977 for £60,000 and was to spend nine years as a Celt. He played over 250 League games for the Glasgow side before moving to Stockport and Hamilton. Motherwell signed him in 1986 and he went on to play over 100 games for Motherwell, all at centre half. His partnership with Craig Paterson was a feature of Tommy McLean's side.

After leaving Motherwell he joined Airdrie and he began his coaching career with the Diamonds before returning to Celtic.

Appearances 98/1 Goals 3

Gary McALLISTER

Sadly, a victim of Motherwell's financial insecurity in the mid-1980s, McAllister was sold before reaching his peak, which came with Leeds United following an exciting spell with Leicester City. Gary went on to be recognised as one of Scotland's foremost midfield talents.

Born in Motherwell in 1964, Gary joined Motherwell from Fir Park Boys' Club in 1981. He made his debut within months and by 1985 was an integral part of the side which won the First Division under the astute leadership of Tommy McLean. His first League goal was certainly a long time coming, in August 1984, against Kilmarnock. Sadly, the financial plight of the club determined that immediate income was vital and both McAllister and Ally Mauchlen were sold to Leicester City just one game into the Premier Division campaign of 1985/86.

The Second Division team briefly sparked with this Scottish influx. McAllister, in particular, caught the eye with a series of cultured performances and he made his full Scotland debut while with the Filbert Street side. Ultimately, his skills brought extensive interest and after turning down Brian Clough and Nottingham Forest, he elected to join Leeds manager Howard Wilkinson for £1million.

In subsequent years Gary won both English First and Second Division Championship medals, and became a midfield fixture in Andy Roxburgh's Scotland plans. By 1993 he was Scotland captain. His goal for Leeds United against Rangers at Ibrox in the famous 'Battle of Britain' European Cup tie in 1992 will be the goal by which many fans remember his career. Sadly, Gary missed a key penalty for Scotland against England at Wembley in the Euro '96 finals and that may well be his future reference point in football circles.

Appearances 53/6 Goals 6

Gary McAllister

Joe McBRIDE

A man of many clubs, his career included stops with Kilmarnock, Wolves, Luton, Partick, Motherwell, Celtic, Hibernian, Dunfermline and Clyde. He was not a success with them all, but was an unqualified success at Fir Park and his departure was as sad as it was inevitable.

His journeys were already well-documented before he arrived in Lanarkshire. In 1957 he went from Rob Roy Juniors to Kilmarnock for £200, and two years later from Killie to Wolves for £12,000. In 1960 he swapped the gold of Wolves for the white of Luton in an £8,000 deal, but returned to Scotland and Partick the same year in exchange for Jim Fleming. His move to Fir Park from Firhill cost £8,000 and Motherwell sold him to Celtic for around £22,000.

McBride came to Fir Park in 1962 from Partick and, although standing at just 5 ft 8 in, he weighed 12 stones and could use his physique to good effect. Razor-sharp around goal and possessed of a clinical football brain, he was deadly in front of goal. He made his debut in a 0-0 draw with Dundee

Joe McBride

United in November and notched up his first goal in a 3-4 defeat at Dunfermline. In his first season as a Steelman he had 11 goals; the very next season he settled in, hitting 19 League goals and supplementing them with an astonishing 15 cup counters.

He was truly established by then and specialised in the hat-trick. Hibs, Falkirk, Dumbarton and Hearts were victims in 1963/64 and in 1964/65 he posted a further 21 League goals and 9 cup scores. Before leaving for Celtic, Joe helped the club land the 1965 Summer Cup by netting against every side Motherwell met. Such prodigious scoring clearly brought its admirers, but there still remains considerable mystery as to how Celtic acquired him for such a paltry fee.

Appearances 88 Goals 51

Martin McBRIDE

A clever winger who was signed from Wishaw Boys' Club in 1984, Martin scored a single goal in 20 League matches. He was eventually granted a free transfer in 1990 and moved on to East Stirlingshire. His solitary Motherwell goal came at the expense of Dundee. He is not to be confused with Stephen McBride, who was on Motherwell's books but made his mark in Northern Ireland with Linfield and Glenavon.

Appearances 15/5 Goals 1

Stephen McBRIDE

A Northern Ireland lad, Stephen began his football in his home town with Hill

Martin McBride

Street Boys' Club, Lurgan. He moved to Belfast club Linfield, where in three years he scored over 60 goals for the reserves, Linfield Swifts. On Christmas Eve 1983 Stephen made a remarkable debut for the Windsor Park senior team, scoring four against Larne. After eight games with Linfield, and five goals, he moved to Fir Park late in January 1984, when he was nineteen years of age, for a transfer fee of £15,000. Bobby Watson quickly introduced him to the Motherwell team when he came on as substitute at Ibrox on 4 February 1984, in a 1-2 defeat. Altogether he was on the bench on five occasions in 1983/84. Following Tommy McLean's arrival as manager, Stephen was allowed to return to Linfield early in 1984/85.

Appearances 0/3 Goals 0

Jim McCabe

Dave MacCABE

An out and out striker, who was snapped up for £40,000 in September 1988 from local rivals Airdrie, Dave never quite reproduced his Airdrie form at Fir Park – in 1985 and 1986 he had scored over 20 goals for the Diamonds. Nevertheless, there was always a certain buzz when Dave was at the heart of a game and he did well with Morton when he moved there in September 1990. Given that he was born in Port Glasgow, a move to Greenock Morton was perhaps the ideal solution for a player who promised so much but delivered so little.

Dave MacCabe

Appearances 12/2 Goals 0

Jim McCABE

Long-haired Jim was recruited from Bargeddie Amateurs in 1969 and occasionally suggested he could be a new McBride or Deans. However, his star gradually waned and he was unable to impose himself on first team football. Nevertheless, he can look back on over a dozen League goals for a

Willie McCall

Motherwell team that was never chasing the honours.

Jim's debut came against Dundee United and he went on to notch up eight goals in what was an impressive first personal campaign. For Texaco Cup matches he was often switched to midfield, and he gave one quite masterly showing in a tie against Hearts. The season of 1972/73 brought 35 appearances with a tally of 7 goals, but by the following campaign he was slipping out of favour and managed only 7 games.

McCabe had a sharp temper, which was amply displayed in the League Cup tie with Clyde at Fir Park in August 1972. On that occasion he celebrated his equalising goal by giving the 'two fingered salute' to Motherwell supporters who had previously barracked him. Manager Howitt fined McCabe and dropped him for two weeks, but the banishment was made more permanent in 1975, when he was granted a free transfer.

Appearances 64/3 Goals 13

Willie McCALL

A dashing outside-left, Willie was signed from Newcastle United in December 1948 for £5,500. He stayed until September 1950, when Motherwell moved him on to Third Lanark for £3,000. His 28 League games in Motherwell's colours brought 8 goals, the most notable of which came in a 4-0 win over Rangers on 10 December 1949. Born in Glasgow in November 1920, he had started his career with Aberdeen.

Appearances 28 Goals 8

Bobby McCALLUM

Signed in 1958 from Bellshill, Bobby remained at Motherwell for nine years and was a reliable if unspectacular full-back. Not always a first choice, he was nevertheless a very dependable player and made over 150 outings.

Bobby McCallum

He scored 9 goals for Motherwell, the bulk of them from the penalty spot. In September 1966 he played for the Scottish League against the League of Ireland at Celtic Park – his only representative honour.

Appearances 157 Goals 9

Willie McCALLUM

A towering centre half, Willie McCallum was signed in 1959 from Douglas Water Thistle, and was by nature a quiet man who went about his business with unswerving loyalty. He stayed at Motherwell for an astonishing length of time – fifteen years – until 1974, when brief spells with St Mirren and Raith Rovers ended his career. He played 277 games for Motherwell and scored a single goal.

Willie's early playing career at Fir Park suffered from being in the shadow of the great John Martis. Indeed, he only got a game when injuries or suspensions left a vacancy. As the 1960s advanced, more opportunities came his way and he proved himself to be up to the challenge. His one goal for Motherwell was a scrambled affair against St Johnstone at Fir Park in 1966. Quiet and unassuming, he was most dependable in an era of change.

Also a gentleman off the field, he was a regular visitor to Motherwell games and a founder committee member of the MFC Former Players' Club.

Appearances 277 Goals 1

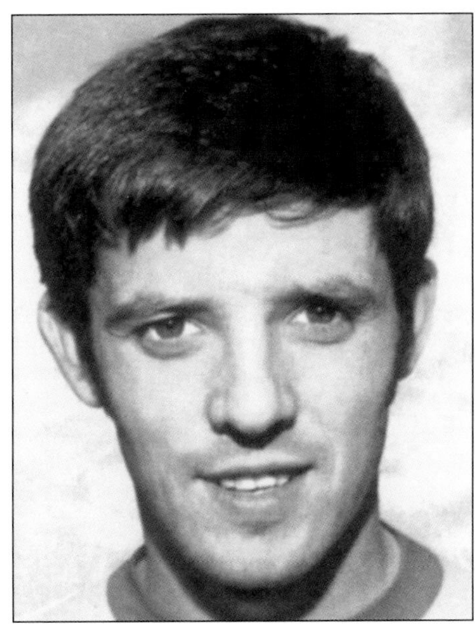
Willie McCallum

Bert McCANN

Signed in 1956 from Queen's Park, Bert stayed with Motherwell until 1965 and played 246 League games. He scored 21 goals in that time and was noted as a clever, gifted player who had both drive and elegance. Indeed Bert was one of the all-time greats at Fir Park and the half-back line of Aitken, Martis and McCann was one of the best in the club's history.

Prior to playing with Queen's Park, Bert was a Dundee United player; indeed he was in the United side that lost 1-12 to Motherwell at Fir Park in Motherwell's record win – and United's record defeat! He won 5 Scotland caps and brought his playing career to an end with a stint at Hamilton Academical. However, there are those who say that Bert's career was effectively ended by a crude tackle in a Scottish Cup semi-final game against Rangers. The Motherwell club doctor at the time said that it was the worst injury he had ever seen, inflicted by studs which had gouged right across Bert's thigh muscle.

In addition to his 5 full Scotland caps he had made 3 Scottish League

Bert McCann

appearances, and played for Motherwell in three losing Scottish Cup semi-finals. Initially he was a part-time player, while studying Modern Languages at Edinburgh University. Before graduating in 1960 he frequently only met his team-mates on a Saturday, even when he was their captain. Amateur, graduate, international and club captain ... Bert was truly a man of many parts!

Appearances 246 Goals 21

Chris McCART

A towering centre half, Chris was a product of the Motherwell youth system and a superb ambassador for the club. A gentleman to the last, he played over 250 League games for Motherwell between 1984 and 1997 and there was genuine surprise amongst the support when he moved to Falkirk. A stalwart of the 1991 Scottish Cup success, he scored a handful of goals for Motherwell but was a true centre half who relied on brain rather than brawn.

Capped by Scotland 'B' against their Welsh counterparts, he scored for both sides in the Wrexham clash of 1994. When Chris left Motherwell in August 1997, it was to join Falkirk. Freed by the Bairns after two seasons, he eventually moved to Celtic in a coaching capacity.

Appearances 260 Goals 6

Brian McCLAIR

In his initial two seasons at Motherwell, Brian McClair was a sensational young player. Plucked from homesickness with Aston Villa in 1981, he broke into the Motherwell side and began to bag goals with regularity. A total of five against the Old Firm in the winter of 1982 really proved his worth. He was sold to Celtic in June 1983 for £75,000 and proved an instant hit at Parkhead.

However, he was too good for the

Chris McCart

Brian McClair

Chic McClelland

Scottish game to hold and ultimately Celtic had to sell him to Manchester United. At Old Trafford he really flourished and helped Alex Ferguson's side to a clutch of honours, as well as advancing his own Scottish international career. He was the first player since George Best to score 20 League goals in a season for United.

He rejoined Motherwell in the summer of 1998 but never quite re-established his old reputation, and when Blackburn Rovers asked him to be their assistant manager he returned to Lancashire.

Appearances 33/7 Goals 15

Chic McCLELLAND

McClelland was signed by Motherwell for £10,000 in 1979 from Aberdeen, where he had enjoyed first team status for most of his six years at Pittodrie. A full-back, easily capable of playing on either side, he liked to get forward and settled in quickly at Fir Park, making 34 League appearances in his first season there. The following season saw Motherwell again struggling unsuccessfully to gain promotion to the Premier Division and McClelland had just fifteen League games before moving on to Dundee at the end of the season.

Appearances 49/2 Goals 1

Peter McCLOY

Despite his eventual success at Ibrox with Rangers, 6 ft 4 in Peter found great difficulty gaining a regular spot at Fir

Peter McCloy

Park and was actually in the reserves when Rangers swooped, in a deal which brought both Bobby Watson and Brian Heron to Fir Park.

From a goalkeeping family, Peter's father had kept goal for St Mirren. Peter joined up from Crosshill Thistle in 1963 as a seventeen-year-old and made his debut under Bobby Howitt in a League game at Morton in the mid-1960s. He saw off the challenge from Alan Wyllie but fared less well against Keith MacRae, despite the latter's insistence on playing outfield whenever possible!

McCloy won a Summer Cup medal in 1965, and his displays en route to the final success over Dundee United were excellent given his youth. His large size – he was nicknamed 'The Girvan Lighthouse' – was a great advantage and his wonderful long clearances a useful weapon against unwary defences. He played against both the Irish Leagues while at Fir Park. Interestingly, although it was Keith MacRae who was remembered as a goalkeeper with a passion for playing outfield, the same could apply to Peter. At Kilmarnock in November 1965, Peter went off injured and returned to play at centre forward – Bobby McCallum going between the sticks – although he could not emulate MacRae by scoring. McCloy joined Rangers in 1970 and won a clutch of honours.

Appearances 137 Goals 0

Willie McCLYMONT

It was from Cumbernauld United that Motherwell signed Willie in 1971. He stayed for four years and played in 48 League games, netting 7 times in the process. A busy player, he had a good finishing instinct but was too often

Willie McClymont

unable to impose his undoubted skills on the game.

Appearances 38/10 Goals 7

Lee McCULLOCH

A towering young striker, Lee was a product of the Fir Park youth system. His early progress was not great, as his initially awkward style allied to ill-fortune around goal made it hard for him to settle. Some of his tackles were both unnecessary and poorly timed, and he tended to pick up a lot of bookings at the start of his career.

However, he slowly but surely developed into a powerful front man and turned the corner when he scored twice in the 6-2 demolition of Hibs at Fir Park. By the late 1990s he was a regular goalscorer and even attracted a huge bid from Hearts. Capped 14 times by Scotland at under-21 level, he proved the perfect foil for the likes of John Spencer and Don Goodman in the Fir Park front-line. He was a decided asset as the club moved into the new millennium.

Appearances 96 Goals 14

Jim McDAID

A New Stevenson lad, McDaid arrived at Fir Park early in the 1966/67 season from Shotts Bon Accord. An outside-left, he made 2 first team appearances that season – against Dundee and Ayr United in October – but on neither occasion did he or Motherwell score.

Appearances 2 Goals 0

Ian MacDONALD

A tenacious midfielder, Ian is perhaps better known for his spell with Partick Thistle than he is for his Motherwell connection. Joining Motherwell in the close season of 1984, he was back at Firhill within six months. He played only 13 games for The Steelmen before his return to Glasgow. Later in his career he joined Morton, and he made a valuable contribution to Allan McGraw's side before joining the Cappielow coaching staff.

Appearances 10/3 Goals 4

Paul McFADDEN

McFadden was yet another who did not realise his potential. A quick, nimble forward, he made his League debut in a rare 2-1 victory over Rangers at Ibrox in October 1983. However, he was unable to build upon that memorable start and was released by Motherwell in 1986. He had been signed in 1982 from Duntocher Boys' Club.

Appearances 12/11 Goals 2

Ian MacFADYEN

Signed from Dundee United in 1954, Ian was the son of the former Motherwell

Paul McFadden

Ian Macfadyen

legend Willie Macfadyen. Willie had later managed Dundee United and it was while he was at Tannadice that he signed Ian. Bobby Ancell convinced Ian to come to Fir Park and he played as both a full-back and an inside forward. He returned to Dundee United five years after joining Motherwell, and helped the Tangerines gain promotion in his first season back at Tannadice.

Appearances 25 Goals 0

Jamie McGOWAN

Signed in 1998 from Falkirk, Jamie was a central defender who could also comfortably fill a full-back position. Yet his stay with Motherwell was to be a short two-year stint. He received a free transfer in the summer of 2000, moving to newly promoted St Mirren.

Born in Morecambe, Jamie had played non-League English football before Dundee signed him. He did well at Dens Park, before moving to Falkirk in a complicated transfer that saw Dragutin Ristic and himself head to Falkirk, while Neil Duffy and Ian Westwater went the other way. It was at Brockville that McGowan really caught the eye, and his inspirational defensive play won him many admirers.

He was adept at many sports, and had represented England at volleyball prior to settling on football.

Appearances 45 Goals 1

Sam McGOWAN

A talented left-winger, Sam played his best football for Motherwell in the war period. Signed from Morton in 1942, he was in the Motherwell side that won the Summer Cup in 1944. He was also a regular in the 1945/46 season, when

Jamie McGowan

Paul McGrillen

he made 27 League appearances out of a possible 30. However, when peace-time football officially got underway in the summer of 1946 he could not break into a Motherwell side that was on the verge of better times. He moved to St Johnstone, but lasted just a single season there, making 18 outings for the Saints.

Appearances 1 Goals 0

Paul McGRILLEN

A pacy little striker, Paul captured the hearts of the Motherwell support with his enormous appetite for the game and optimistic attitude. Goals took a long time to arrive but he was making steady progress, and had won two Under-21 caps when he was moved to Falkirk along with Stevie Kirk in the deal that brought the versatile Eddie May to Motherwell. Paul then played for Falkirk and Airdrie before he continued his senior career by teaming up with former team-mate John Philliben at Stirling Albion, when the latter was the Albion boss. Signed in 1990 from Motherwell BC, he departed in February 1995.

Appearances 87 Goals 13

Bobby McGUINNESS

Signed in 1973 from Lesmahagow Juniors, Bobby was a centre half. He started four matches and played four more as a substitute before being released in 1975.

Appearances 4/4 Goals 0

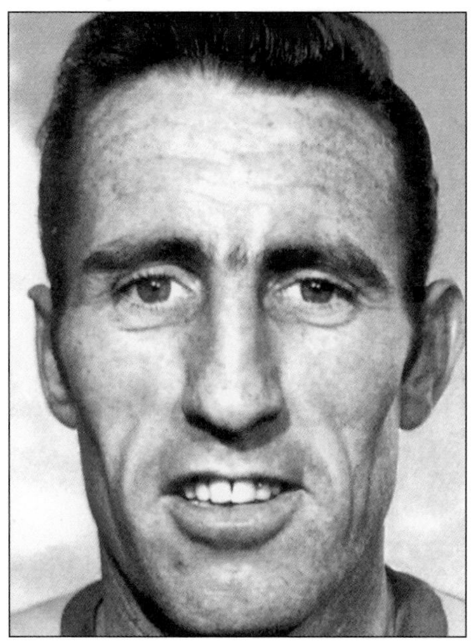

Jackie McInally

Jim McILWRAITH

Jim only started playing football when he was fifteen but made rapid progress. Playing for Troon Juniors, he was signed by Kilwinning when he was eighteen and the very next season emerged as one of junior football's most prolific goalscorers, with a haul of over 60 to his credit. Ian St John was quick to note his potential and Jim signed for Motherwell in October 1973.

In 1974/75 he made 18 League appearances for Motherwell and 5 in the Scottish Cup. Initially he remained a part-timer, keeping his job as an apprentice fabricator, until he became a full-time professional in January 1975. In September 1975 he moved to the Lancashire side Bury, in a deal which brought George Buchan to Fir Park on a month's trial, with a view to the deal becoming permanent.

Jim's skill made him an instant success at Gigg Lane, but when the proposed deal fell through he returned to Fir Park, where his popularity continued. However, competition for first team places was keen and when the opportunity arose, Jim moved permanently to Bury a few weeks later. His last goal for Motherwell was in a 2-1 victory over Dundee United on 22 November 1975. He eventually played for Bury and Portsmouth before spending a month on loan at Ayr United, where he once again teamed up with manager Willie McLean.

Appearances 21/7 Goals 5

Jackie McINALLY

Powerful and direct, McInally made his name at Kilmarnock, where he not only won a League Championship medal but played in several European fixtures and scored 127 goals in just 287 matches. Motherwell paid £5,000 for his services in March 1968 and his wide experience was ideally suited to orchestrating the younger players around him. His aggressive style, allied to his tall frame, quickly won over the Motherwell support, and his goals per game ratio proved his success. His spectacular overhead kick at East End Park in October 1970 to win the game for Motherwell will be long remembered by those privileged to see it. He moved to Hamilton Accies on a free transfer in 1973.

Appearances 134 Goals 37

Jim McINTYRE

Signed from Forth Wanderers in 1953, Jim made a dozen outings for Motherwell but was unable to oust Hastie Weir from the regular spot. He left in 1956, apparently intent on playing non-League football in England.

Appearances 12 Goals 0

John McKEEVER

A dashing little forward, John McKeever's career promised much, but ultimately failed to deliver. In the early 1980s he burst into the first team with a flash of inspiration and his two-goal performance against Hearts in a pulsating 2-2 draw in October 1981 at Fir Park suggested a glittering career lay ahead. Alas, it was not to be and John, like many a promising youngster before him, drifted from the scene and was eventually allowed to leave Fir Park on a free transfer in 1982.

Appearances 14/8 Goals 7

Kevin McKEOWN

A powerful goalkeeper, Kevin played only a handful of games for the club before moving to Northern Ireland and trying his luck in the Northern Irish League. He did reasonably well there and made his mark at several clubs. The highlight of his stay might well have been helping little Crusaders win two League championships.

Appearances 3 Goals 0

Rab McKINNON

A left-sided defender, Rab was snapped up from Hartlepool United in January 1992 for £125,000, having made his name there after a short and unsuccessful spell with Newcastle United.

Prior to his stint at Motherwell, Rab had served his soccer apprenticeship in the Juniors with Rutherglen Glencairn before going south to Newcastle United in 1984. He made only one League outing for the Magpies before joining Hartlepool.

He proved to be one of Tommy McLean's most astute signings. Strong and athletic, he played with speed and directness and in the era of overlapping full-backs shone brightly in the Motherwell side. Indeed, he shone so much that he was one of the first Bosman problems to hit the club. On the verge of playing for Scotland, he was lured away to Twente Enschede of Holland in July 1996 under the Bosman ruling, with Motherwell receiving absolutely nothing. He did not do as well in the Netherlands as he had in Lanarkshire and returned to Scotland with Hearts in July 1998.

Appearances 144 Goals 8

Stewart McLAREN

A classic example of the utility player, Stewart McLaren was a key figure in the powerful Motherwell side of the mid-to late-1970s. His versatility was exploited in both defence and midfield and he brought a never-ending commitment and enthusiasm to Fir Park for four years. In 1978 he moved to Dundee and later finished his career with Hearts in 1984. In a career that had spanned sixteen years, he was always a full-time professional and would have won a handful of honours but for some dreadful luck.

A native of Larkhall, Stewart was an impressive amateur player, so much so that he signed for the top ranking English side West Bromwich Albion when only sixteen. Despite captaining both their youth and reserve sides, he never quite made the breakthrough into the Midland club's senior team and returned home.

Motherwell manager Ian St John beat

Rab McKinnon

offers from Dunfermline and Falkirk for Stewart. At Fir Park, all of the player's early potential came to fruition. Playing as a midfield anchor man, he quickly established himself in the first team and helped Motherwell secure a spot in the first ever Premier Division. Under Willie McLean's guidance the club embarked upon a run that took them to fourth spot in the League and the verge of European football.

It would be impossible to overlook the fact that this Motherwell side was known for its uncompromising, some would say hard, style. McLaren, along with Peter Millar, Gregor Stevens, Willie McVie and Willie Watson evolved into a strong defence that seemed capable of striking fear into opposing forward lines.

Yet, despite the strong reputation the club had built, it was destined to underachieve. In 1975 local rivals Airdrie administered a surprise Scottish Cup semi-final exit, and tragically it was an own goal by Stewart that sealed the result. The following year the club went even closer to the final, leading Rangers 2-0 at half time in a pulsating semi-final. The Ibrox club rallied after the interval and squeezed home 3-2 following a dubious penalty.

In 1978 Stewart left for Dundee, sold by ex-Rangers player Roger Hynd to former Celtic legend Tommy Gemmell. For a fee of just £30,000 the Dens Park side got a player whose enthusiasm was a major factor in their victory in the First Division Championship in 1979. In 1981 they again achieved promotion, but in the interim, in addition to experiencing relegation, Stewart had missed the League Cup final when he fractured his cheekbone in a successful semi-final against Ayr United.

McLaren's career ended with Hearts under Alex MacDonald. A Hearts revival with veterans such as Jimmy Bone, Sandy Jardine and Willie Johnston gave the Maroons a purple patch, which brought not only promotion but European

Stewart McLaren

football too. A recurring pelvic injury allied to back problems eventually ended McLaren's career. Throughout, he had displayed a courage and forcefulness that epitomised the side of Willie McLean at Fir Park.

Appearances 117/6 Goals 4

Brian McLAUGHLIN

Brian joined Celtic from schools' football, becoming a full-time professional in 1971. The marvellous Celtic side of that era, inspired by the legendary Jock Stein, went on to win nine successive League titles, and Brian starred in the reserves alongside Kenny Dalglish and Lou Macari. He eventually made his debut against Clydebank in September 1972 and by the following year had established himself in the first team. No less an opinion than that of Jock Stein

Brian McLaughlin

noted that 'Brian McLaughlin was the most naturally talented player he had ever signed'.

Disaster struck after fourteen successive appearances when he was badly injured against Clyde. The cruciate ligament damage removed him from the game for two years and although he fought back gamely he lacked his previous mobility and was released to Ayr United in November 1977.

Those who had considered him to be finished misjudged his great determination. Incredibly, he had two good seasons with Ayr and even scored the winning goal when United defeated Celtic 2-1 on 31 December 1977. The quality of his play at Somerset Park was rewarded by the Players' First Division Player of the Year award in 1979. A £100,000 transfer fee then brought him to Fir Park where his midfield skills made him a firm favourite with the fans. Suddenly Motherwell became a free scoring machine, with Brian orchestrating everything from midfield. Motherwell were promoted to the Premier League in 1982 and Brian was voted Players' First Division Player of the Year for the second time.

Unfortunately, after the appointment of Jock Wallace as manager Brian was quickly transferred to Hamilton Academical for £25,000 in 1983. The magnitude of this mistake was immediately apparent, as Brian quickly played a leading role in transforming Accies into an attractive side. He then moved on to Falkirk for two seasons, followed by a year in Australia. On returning to Scotland he had a final season with Ayr United before retiring from the game in the summer of 1987.

What a player Brian might have been had it not been for that cruel injury! Few could match him for skill, and the boy who was a teenage sensation with Celtic in the early 1970s might have gone on to grace the world's premier football stages.

Appearances 108/8 Goals 37

John McLAUGHLIN

John made his League bow early in the 1965/66 season. Flitting across the forward line he was soon amongst the goals, with strikes against Hamilton, Partick and Hearts coming early in his career. However, he could not sustain that promising start and ended the campaign with 4 goals from 18 starts. This was not enough to earn a permanent place at Fir Park.

Appearances 18 Goals 4

Alistair McLEAN

A goalkeeper signed from Aberdeen in 1980 and one of Motherwell's one-game wonder players, Alistair was unfortunate at both Motherwell and Aberdeen in that good goalkeepers were surprisingly aplenty. He was unable to dislodge Hugh Sproat from the number 1 position and left in 1981.

Prior to playing with Aberdeen he was with Ayr United, whom he had joined in 1971. Indeed, he played under Ally MacLeod at three different clubs: Ayr, Aberdeen and Motherwell. Amongst his other clubs were St Mirren, Cumnock Juniors and Irvine Meadow. When his playing days ended he became assistant manager to Alex McAnespie at Stranraer.

Appearances 1 Goals 0

Paul McLEAN

Were it not for a broken leg, Paul McLean would surely have made his mark at Motherwell. Signed by Tommy McLean from Queen's Park in 1989, he was said to be on the verge of great things when his broken leg intervened. As it was he made two brief outings as a substitute early in the 1989/90 campaign and then moved on to Ayr United in June 1991. He enjoyed greater success at Somerset Park but moved to Stranraer in October 1992.

Appearances 0/2 Goals 0

Alex McLEISH

Make no mistake, as a player Alex McLeish was at the very top of the Scottish tree. Capped 77 times by Scotland, he served Aberdeen with distinction for a staggering eighteen years. And those were no ordinary eighteen years as his honours roll proves – a Cup Winners Cup medal, 3 Premier League badges, a Super Cup winner's medal, 5 Scottish Cup winner's medals, 2 League Cup gongs and 458 League games tucked under the belt. What got Alex to the top was the desire to be a winner.

Born in Glasgow, Alex went to school in the Kinning Park district before his parents moved to Barrhead. His senior education was gained in Barrhead and Paisley and at one point an engineering apprenticeship with Rolls Royce looked possible until football beckoned. An apprenticeship with Aberdeen was too good to turn down, and so it was off to the Granite City for Alex.

It was John McNab, an Aberdeen scout, who had sent Alex from Glasgow United to Pittodrie in 1976. Ally MacLeod was in charge then, but it was under the guidance of first Billy McNeill, and then the magnificent Alex Ferguson, that young Alex McLeish established his wonderful reputation. His debut came in a 1-0 win over Dundee United in

Alex McLeish

January 1978, and a few months later his legendary partnership with Willie Miller, in the heart of the Aberdeen defence, was cemented.

In 1980 the name McLeish made its first appearance in the Scotland senior ranks, Portugal providing the opposition. By December 1987 he had registered 50 full caps, and by the time he had reached 77, he had played alongside his Aberdeen team-mate Willie Miller in a staggering 48 internationals.

The Football Writers' Player of the Year in 1990, he earned total respect as a player. By the early 1990s he had gained all of his coaching certificates, and it was clear he would be able to offer a lot to any coaching post.

The opening came at Motherwell in the wake of Tommy McLean's departure. Although in essence a player-manager, he played only two Premier League matches in Motherwell's colours, preferring to concentrate on coaching. He was Motherwell's twelfth manager, and his friendly manner allied to his excellent knowledge of the game made him a very popular figure. It would also be fair to say he was considerably 'warmer' with the public and press than Tommy McLean.

Hibernian were amongst those clubs who quietly but with interest noticed the progress of Alex in the coaching world. When Motherwell defeated Hibernian 6-2 in a key relegation match in January 1998, Hibs made their move and Alex made his – he took Andy Watson, the Motherwell assistant manager, to Easter Road with him.

Appearances 2 Goals 0

Steve McLelland

Steve McLELLAND

Although born in Aberdeen, Steve signed from Ayr United in January 1980 and was 'pitchforked' into the senior side as a striker. However, despite an early run in the side, he was unable to establish himself. Then he was played as sweeper in January 1981 and never looked back.

At 6ft tall and weighing 12 stones, he was ideal for the heart of the defence, as he was also quick and very strong in the tackle. He was one of the stars in Motherwell's First Division Championship-winning side, making 36 League appearances. Unfortunately, he only had three Premier starts the following season as a defender before Jock Wallace switched him back to striker, where he made eleven appearances, plus one as substitute at Tannadice in December 1982 as Motherwell were hammered 0-5. This proved to be his last game in Motherwell's colours and he moved on at the end of the season.

He was a player who probably suffered more than most from a change of management at Fir Park. If David Hay had remained, Steve would no doubt have had many more appearances to his name. He had played at junior level with Largs Thistle prior to playing with Ayr United.

Appearances 78/1 Goals 7

Donald McLEOD

There were few more loyal servants to Motherwell than Donald McLeod. Edinburgh born, he came to Motherwell in 1938 from Whitburn Juniors and stayed for thirteen years. Were it not for the plethora of excellent Motherwell defenders on the books at that time, he would surely have amassed more outings.

Tall and with great stamina, Donald was a right-half to remember. A tremendous one-club man, it is probably true to say that his finest hour for Motherwell was in the side which won the Scottish League Cup in 1950/51. The arrival of Charlie Cox finally eclipsed his Fir Park career, although he was a losing Scottish Cup finalist in 1951 against Celtic. A fully qualified engineer, he moved to Hearts in 1951 to be their assistant trainer.

Appearances 127 Goals 1

Ian MacLEOD

A native of East Kilbride, Ian played his early football with the prestigious East Kilbride amateur side Claremont. He was offered full-time football by Dundee United aged seventeen, but after careful consideration turned this offer down because he was keen to continue his Business Studies degree at Glasgow Polytechnic. United boss Jim McLean was so impressed by this attitude that he tipped off his brother Willie, then Motherwell boss, about the talent on his doorstep. Thus, in 1977, Ian signed for Motherwell.

Ian MacLeod

For his first four years at Motherwell Ian continued his studies and he made his first team debut at Partick Thistle in March 1979. He quickly became a favourite with the Fir Park support, mainly because of his wholehearted style of play and his fierce, uncompromising tackling. He went on to serve nine Motherwell managers in all, including Ally MacLeod, Davie Hay and Tommy McLean. He won a First Division championship badge in 1982 with Davie Hay, and in 1985 added another under Tommy McLean.

Ian always put his Business Studies degree to good use. He was employed by the Edinburgh-based Ferranti company while at Fir Park, and carried out his part-time training schedules

Joe McLeod

with Falkirk. It was therefore perhaps understandable that he duly left for Falkirk just after his twenty-seventh birthday. That transfer, in 1986, cost Falkirk £20,000.

From Falkirk he moved to Raith Rovers, where he made himself indispensable at full-back. He had the rare gift of being able to play either left or right-back. He even popped up with the odd goal, one counter coming at Montrose in 1992. An extremely fit man, his lengthy career had been testimony to his enormous dedication. The man behind his move to Raith had been Frank Connor, who had been assistant boss at Motherwell when Ian was there.

It was fitting then that Ian should add to his two Motherwell First Division badges in 1993, when Raith Rovers won the First Division title. With 243 League games for Motherwell, over 150 for Raith and 68 for Falkirk, Ian clearly played his career to the full.

Appearances 236/7 Goals 3

Joe McLEOD

Signed by Tommy McLean in September 1990 from his brother, Jim, at Dundee United, Joe arrived with a solid reputation as a free-scoring Dundee United reserve. Alas, he could not transfer that success to the Motherwell first team and his major contribution was a goal against Falkirk in Motherwell's cup winning season. Joe netted only one League goal, against St Johnstone, and never enjoyed the support of the Motherwell fans. He was allowed to join Stirling Albion after a stint on loan to Portadown and also played for a spell with Berwick Rangers.

Appearances 23/23 Goals 1

Mick McMANUS

A small and pacy winger who joined Motherwell in 1975 from Ashfield Juniors, Mick never really established himself at Motherwell and moved to Hamilton Accies in 1977, where he flourished. He reached double figures for them in the 1977/78 season, showing a good eye for goal.

Appearances 1/2 Goals 0

Stephen McMILLAN

A powerful young full-back, Stephen broke into the Motherwell first team as a teenager and soon made a name for himself with a series of energetic displays. A product of the club's own youth system, his debut came in the final fixture of the 1993/94 season against St Johnstone. Thereafter, he gradually staked his claim to a first eleven spot.

He made an impression that spread

far wider than Fir Park and in 1997 he won four Scotland Under-21 caps. Moreover, he was soon the subject of transfer speculation. Sadly, this saw his form dip a little, but by the time the Millennium arrived he was back to his best. He was displaying quite an eye for goal from direct free kicks around the opposition box, and he scored a useful 3 goals in the 1999/2000 season.

Appearances 127 Goals 6

Colin McNAIR

The less said about the career of Colin McNair at Fir Park the better, perhaps. A strong, young defender signed from Falkirk in 1989, he lashed out at Jim Griffin so violently in training that Jim was badly injured. Tommy McLean sacked Colin instantly, and he rejoined Falkirk shortly afterwards.

Appearances 1/1 Goals 0

Stephen McMillan

John McPhee

John McNEIL

John was with Hibs in the early 1950s, when they had a fine side, and he found himself unable to break into the first team. He was signed from the Hibees as an inside left and made 5 League appearances for Motherwell in 1954/55, as a wing-half. With Charlie Cox and Willie Redpath still playing, opportunities were obviously going to be rare, especially as Wilson Humphries, Jim Forrest and Charlie Aitken were also to the fore. McNeil was released at the end of the 1955 season.

Appearances 5 Goals 0

John McPHEE

One of the later batch of 'Ancell Babes', John was an elegant midfielder with a flair for getting forward and scoring goals. Signed from Douglas Water Thistle in 1957, he stayed at Motherwell for five seasons and in that time was one of the

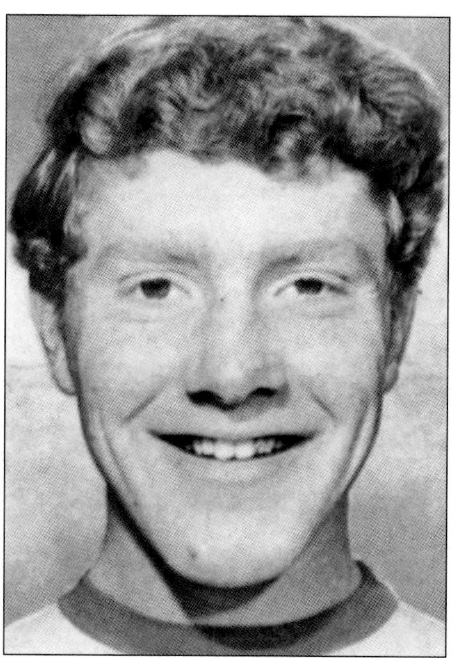

Keith MacRae

more influential Fir Park players. He scored in the 5-2 cup rout of Rangers at Ibrox in March 1961 and consistently impressed with his work rate. Watched enviously by several other clubs, he was eventually sold to Blackpool in August 1962 for £10,000 as Ancell struggled to hold on to his talented young squad in the face of rich earnings in England.

McPhee was versatile and could play both on the wing and as a centre. He was given a benefit just before his transfer to Blackpool – where he was, conveniently enough, already a partner in a hotel! He made 250 outings for Blackpool between 1962 and 1969, before moving on to Barnsley and then Southport.

Appearances 74 Goals 16

Keith MacRAE

One of the more remarkable players to have represented Motherwell, Keith MacRae was a goalkeeper who frankly 'fancied' himself as a bit of an outfield player too. And it was no idle boast on his part. So useful was he that Bobby Howitt fielded him as a forward on a couple of occasions, and Keith responded by scoring!

Signed from Lanark Grammar School, he had already been capped by the Scottish Professional Youth team and would soon add Scotland under-23 and League caps to his collection. Keith went on to make 119 League appearances for Motherwell, not all of them being confined to goalkeeping duties. However, as his time at the club coincided with that of Peter McCloy, another splendid goalkeeper, Motherwell were in a quandary. Either of them could be used as a substitute, in the days when only one sub was permitted. For MacRae this was a great solution.

An agile performer, he was also a great shot-stopper and, although not the biggest of custodians, he could be relied upon to dominate his area. His performances were good and he quickly attracted the interest of international selectors and other clubs. Eventually he moved to Manchester City, then the pride of that city, for a six figure sum in 1973. Sadly, his English career never quite took off, and he moved to America following a brief stint with Leeds United.

Appearances 119 Goals 1

Willie McROBERTS

McRoberts was a winger who came close to breaking into the immediate post war Motherwell side. However, he ultimately could not hold down a regular spot and, like Sammy McGowan, moved on to St Johnstone. In Willie's case the move to Perth came in 1948.

Appearances 5 Goals 2

Willie McSEVENEY

Willie joined Dunfermline in September 1948 from Wishaw Juniors. He was nineteen at the time and quickly became a first team regular, playing as an inside forward and wing-half. He made his Pars debut in a 1-0 League Cup win over Rangers and lashed a 40 yarder against the underside of the bar in a promising bow.

Willie was sold to Motherwell by none other than Bobby Ancell, who was the Pars boss at the time. He was a £1,200 purchase in March 1953, when both sides were in Division 'B', and for the Pars the move came four years after they had rejected a £4,500 offer from Middlesbrough.

In four games in the 'B' League he hit four goals for Motherwell, including a debut goal in a 1-1 draw with Third Lanark, which ensured promotion. The following season he played in the Motherwell side beaten by Hearts in the League Cup final, and he went on to play for the club in two Scottish Cup semi-final defeats.

A versatile performer, the only two jerseys he did not wear at Fir Park were the goalkeeper's and that of outside-left. He scored goals at centre forward and managed two at left-back in a game against Dundee United in 1961.

Willie enjoyed ten years at Fir Park and upon his retirement he coached the reserve side, helping to nurture young talent such as Joe Wark, Keith MacRae and Peter McCloy. Willie's fundamental philosophy was that players should be allowed to express their individual skills. He is still to be seen around Fir Park in his work with the Former Players' Club.

Appearances 197 Goals 20

Shaun McSKIMMING

Alex McLeish spent a Motherwell record fee of £350,000 to bring Shuan McSkimming to Fir Park in November 1994. Motherwell were top of the League at the time and McSkimming was seen as a valuable addition to a squad that was already quite strong. However, the silky skills of Shaun were never fully appreciated by the Motherwell faithful, who were perhaps perplexed by his casual style. Signed from Kilmarnock, he was a left sided player capable of playing in midfield or as a full-back; he was also a useful goalscorer, all of which makes his lack of popularity hard to understand.

What hampered Shaun more than anything at Fir Park was surely his run of injuries, which in effect reduced his Motherwell career to a series of

Willie McSeveney

Shaun McSkimming

awkward fits and starts. He started his career with Stranraer, then moved to Dundee before joining Kilmarnock. From Motherwell he went back to Dundee in 1999, where his honest endeavour was much appreciated and he fitted in well.

Appearances 64 Goals 7

John McSTAY

A member of the well known McStay clan – of whom cousin Paul at Celtic was the best known – John joined Motherwell as a youngster from Gartcosh United in 1982 and gave a handful of fairly sound displays. He made his debut at Bayview in January 1985, in a 2-1 victory over East Fife, but was never able to command a run in the first team. He moved on to Raith Rovers in July 1987.

It was while he was with Raith Rovers that he was catapulted into the national news. Head-butted by Duncan Ferguson of Rangers during a match at Ibrox, the Rangers player, who had had brushes with both the footballing and civil authorities in his recent history, was subsequently given a lengthy ban and jailed.

John later served Clydebank, East Fife, Ayr United, Clyde and Albion Rovers. His dad's uncle was the legendary Willie McStay of Celtic fame.

Appearances 11/9 Goals 1

Willie McVIE

Willie McVie was uncompromising. He was, in footballing terminology, something of a 'hard man'. A centre half, he had the build and aggression to shackle most forwards and did not take kindly to defeat. Few who saw him in action forgot him.

From humble beginnings with Lesmahagow Juniors, Willie joined Archie Robertson's Clyde and spent over five years at Shawfield. In 1975 Willie McLean signed him for Motherwell for £35,000, and he added much-needed

Willie McVie

muscle to the Fir Park rearguard.

He moved to the embryonic American Football League in 1979, along with fellow 'war-horses' Drew Busby and Jimmy Bone, signing for the quaintly named Toronto Blizzard, but was persuaded to return to Hearts by Bobby Moncur. His career ended at Blantyre Victoria, and in 1982 he won a Scottish Junior Cup medal.

Appearances 85/2 Goals 2

Rob MAASKANT

One of Tommy McLean's excursions into the European market saw him sign huge central defender Rob Maskaant, although it should be noted that Rob's father was the football agent who linked Sieb Dykstra to Fir Park. For a while Rob looked as if he might just make a mark at Motherwell, but in truth he lacked the pace or, in its absence, the exceptional redeeming qualities, to cut the ice in the Premier League and he left after a dozen fairly uneventful appearances. He was one of four Dutch players at the club in the 1991/92 campaign, the others being Luc Nijholt, Bart Verheul and Sieb Dykstra. When Maaskant left Motherwell it was to join Go Ahead Eagles Deventer. Rob had been signed from Emmen in July 1991 and was released twelve months later.

Appearances 12 Goals 0

John MACKAY

In 1978 John was signed from Hillwood Boys Club in nearby Hamilton. He was a player who initially promised much in either midfield or at the back. Making his League debut in 1980/81, he seemed to be finding his feet in the championship winning side of 1981/82, but he was injured and missed much of the season. He did not feature in the senior side at all in the 1982/83 campaign and was released at the end of it.

Appearances 17/1 Goals 0

Alan MACKIN

Alan's senior career began at Queen's Park, where his huge frame and no-nonsense style of defending earned him cult status. In 1978 the Spiders defeated Motherwell 3-1 at Fir Park in a Scottish Cup upset and Mackin gave an outstanding display. He joined Motherwell soon afterwards and immediately set about proving his worth at a higher level. However, he played just 17 League games for Motherwell before falling out with Motherwell boss Ally MacLeod. The dispute gave

Rob Maaskant

Scottish football one of its all-time great newspaper interviews. When asked whom he would most like to meet, Mackin responded in rather unorthodox fashion – 'Ally MacLeod ... in a dark alley'. Given that he stood at 6 ft 2 in and weighed in at just under 13 st, this was no mean prospect from a man who was occasionally known to be a bit of a joker and a character!

His reputation as a rather hard player was thus cemented. He moved, not surprisingly, from Motherwell and went to serve Falkirk, Morton, Partick Thistle, Queen of the South, East Stirling and Clyde. Alan was ultimately a director at East Stirling and had business interests which included a glass merchants firm. Interestingly, his son, also Alan, became a noted tennis player, reaching a very high standard indeed in 1999.

Appearances 15/2 Goals 0

Joe MACKIN

Joe Mackin's story at Fir Park was remarkable. Released at the end of the 1958/59 season, he was recruited by Motherwell again at the beginning of 1959/60 because of a 'keeper crisis in the reserves. He played so well that he was promoted to the senior side, making 20 appearances and earning great popularity with the fans. At the end of the season he was the Supporters' Club Player of the Year but was almost immediately released again to join Carlisle United, as Frank Duncan and Alan Wyllie had returned from the Forces to join Hastie Weir as the goalkeeping complement.

Mackin really began his career with Muirkirk Juniors, although he had actually spent a season with Morton by this stage. He turned senior again with Dunfermline Athletic, and in December 1957 joined Ayr United. It was from the Honest Men that he came to Fir Park in 1958 and he left for the second time in 1960. He died in 1990.

Appearances 20 Goals 0

David MAIN

Motherwell beat a flock of Scottish and English clubs for the signature of this local boy in April 1970. He had won several schoolboy and amateur honours as a full-back, but had early games for Motherwell in midfield. Unfortunately, David was another wonderful schoolboy who failed to establish himself in the claret and amber. He moved to Albion Rovers in 1974.

Appearances 17/2 Goals 2

Gordon MAIR

A slightly-built winger, Gordon had a few clubs in his career and stayed with Motherwell for a couple of seasons.

Gordon Mair

Fairly quick and capable of delivering a useful cross, he suffered from the wingers' malaise – lack of consistency. He was signed in the summer of 1986 from Lincoln City, but had been with Fir Park BC before moving south to join Notts County. From Motherwell he went to Clydebank in 1990, and then former Motherwell defender George Burley signed him for Ayr United.

Appearances 49/2 Goals 2

Andy MANN

Andy joined the ranks of the one game wonders at Fir Park when he played against Dunfermline in a 1-2 reversal in the 1961/62 season. At the end of this season he was freed by Motherwell and moved the short distance to Hamilton Accies. He made nearly fifty outings for the Douglas Park club before receiving his second free transfer.

Appearances 1 Goals 0

Peter MARINELLO

A dazzling winger, Peter was a teenage sensation with Hibernian and earned a £100,000 transfer to Arsenal. He was hailed in London as 'the new George Best' and that proved a tag he could never live up to. Following an unhappy stint at Portsmouth he joined Motherwell in 1975 and settled to a sound game.

Ironically, he made his Motherwell debut at Easter Road against Hibernian. He was to play a huge part in the club's run to the Scottish Cup semi-finals in 1976 during which they defeated Hibernian in a twice replayed quarter-final tie. He still had occasional flashes of genius and was an exciting player. After two seasons he was on the move again, this time back to London and the less demanding environs of Fulham, but he did come back to Scotland and played with Hearts for a short time. Ultimately, he was a player who promised much more than he delivered.

Appearances 77/12 Goals 11

Peter Marinello

Alex MARTIN

Alex joined Hull from Lothians underage football, and spent three and a half years on Humberside before joining Motherwell on the recommendation of Hull City's chief scout John McSeveney – brother of Motherwell's Willie. Despite his pace and trickery, either on the wing or in midfield, he was unable to have a prolonged run in the side and was freed in 1975.

Appearances 61/6 Goals 8

Brian MARTIN

At his peak, Brian Martin was a wonderful defender; indeed, he won two Scotland

Brian Martin

caps while at Motherwell. Not by any means quick, his game was built around exceptional 'reading' of events and a wonderful sense of commitment. Signed by Tommy McLean in November 1991 from St Mirren, he cost £175,000 but proved a sound investment and played over 250 games for Motherwell. His career had started nearby at Albion Rovers before stints with Shotts, Stenhousemuir, Falkirk, Hamilton and St Mirren followed. The potential he had displayed at those clubs came to fruition at Fir Park.

It was sad that Brian ultimately left the club under a cloud, having criticised them in the national press. He moved to Stirling Albion, where his long time defensive partner John Philliben was boss. Indeed, it was a side with many Motherwell connections, given that Ally Graham and young 'keeper Garry Gow were also there. From Stirling he eventually moved on to John Lambie's Partick Thistle.

Appearances 237 Goals 10

John MARTIS

With 297 League outings to his name, the importance of John Martis to Motherwell is crystal clear. His greatest legacy is that he proved to be an admirable replacement for the legendary Andy Paton – no mean accolade. Signed from Royal Albert – the Larkhall based Junior side – in 1957, John was an out and out centre half. He was powerful and determined, and went on to win Scotland caps at both senior and Under-23 level.

A memorable career began with a degree of challenge, for John found himself up against Hibernian's heroic

John Martis

centre forward Joe Baker in his very first game. He clearly benefited from that baptism of fire, as he went on to spend twelve years at Fir Park and was one of the heroes of the 5-2 Scottish Cup win at Ibrox. While the diminutive forward line of the 'Ancell Babes' frequently got the headlines, John was the rock in defence and often an unsung hero. He played in each of the four victories over Rangers in the 1959/60 season.

He quit Motherwell in January 1969 and played with Cape Town-based Hellenic in South Africa, before returning to resume his career with East Fife. This proved a success and John played for six years at Bayview, before eventually managing the Methil club – at one point former team-mate Pat Quinn was his assistant. When he did

Davie Mathie

give up on football, he concentrated on his plumbing business.
Appearances 297 Goals 2

Willie MASON
Signed as a twenty-three-year-old from Linlithgow Rose in 1954, Willie was a tall defender who had completed his National Service before joining Motherwell. Football ran in his family, as his father George had played for St Mirren, Falkirk and St Johnstone. Andy Paton was in possession of the number five jersey, but Willie took his chances to stand in. He played briefly for Accies after leaving Motherwell in 1956, but was freed within a year of moving to Douglas Park.
Appearances 26 Goals 0

Davie MATHIE
Mathie was a nineteen-year-old steelworker when he signed from Wishaw Juniors in 1938. Centre forward Davie is in that small category of players who played for Motherwell before and after the Second World War. He quickly revealed himself to be a prolific marksman. A strong little striker, he could bag the goals with ease and he was hugely popular at Fir Park. In 1945 he moved to Clyde and from Shawfield his travels next took him to Partick Thistle. Motherwell bought him from there for £2,725. His Fir Park career finally ended in 1951, when he was released by the club. He thereafter took his goalscoring tricks to Kilmarnock and bagged 20 for Killie in the 1951/52 season. During the war Davie served with the Cameronians.
Appearances 31/2 Goals 15

Rob MATTHAEI
This Dutch midfielder was a fair player but found problems breaking into the Motherwell team. Signed in the summer of

Rob Matthaei

1998, he could hold the ball up and had good vision, but of all the Harri Kampman signings this was the most mysterious, in that he just did not seem to fit in. Capped by Holland at both Under-18 and Under-21 levels, it was clear that he had talent. Stints with Haarlem, De Graafshad and Volendaam preceded his spell at Motherwell. Matthae found himself on the sidelines for the duration of his stay at Motherwell when Billy Davies was manager. Eventually, in the summer of 2000, his contract expired and he swiftly moved to Dunfermline, where he rejoined fellow Dutchman Michel Doesburg.

Appearances 16/4 Goals 0

Ally MAUCHLEN

At one time the Motherwell captain, Mauchlen developed from an aggressive midfielder into a player who could organise those around him. Alas, this quality was noticed by several other clubs and he left just one game into Motherwell's return to the Premier League when Leicester City signed both Mauchlen and McAllister in a joint deal worth some £250,000.

Ally Mauchlen

Ally Maxwell

Ally joined Kilmarnock in 1978 from Irvine Meadow and made well over 100 appearances for the Rugby Park club. His move to Motherwell took place in 1982 and, together with McAllister and Walker, he helped the club secure Premier status in 1985. An inspirational leader, he was club captain by 1984 and appeared in 29 League matches in the successful promotion campaign. Very successful in England, he did come back to Scotland, but in the colours of Hearts. He later played in Northern Ireland with Glenavon.

Appearances 75/1 Goals 4

Ally MAXWELL

Born in Hamilton, Maxwell joined

M

Eddie May

Motherwell in 1981 from Fir Park Boys' Club. He was slow to break into the first team, but ultimately made the number 1 jersey his own. His highlight at Fir Park is easily identifiable – the 1991 Scottish Cup final. Against Dundee United he gave a supremely brave performance, soldiering on when so badly injured that he spent the evening after the game in hospital.

Remarkably, that match was his final outing for Motherwell. He quickly found himself in a contractual dispute and was sidelined until April 1992, when he moved to Rangers. His next move was to Dundee United, where another former Motherwell custodian, Sieb Dykstra, was in possession. In 1998 Ally joined Greenock Morton and gave manager Billy Stark sound service.

Appearances 134 Goals 0

Eddie MAY

A versatile little player, Eddie began his career with Hibernian and was one of their more promising youngsters. He moved to Brentford in a deal worth £165,000 and only came back to Scotland when Jim Jefferies of Falkirk showed an interest. It was Alex McLeish who signed him for Motherwell, giving Stevie Kirk, Paul McGrillen, and a reputed fee of £150,000 to the Bairns in exchange. It was a deal which, given Kirk's enormous popularity, was something of a mill-stone around May's neck.

In fairness to May, he proved himself a hard-working player but he was no Stevie Kirk and always appeared hindered by the nature of his transfer. He gave sterling displays at both full-back and in midfield, but criticism was never far away. He moved to Dunfermline in August 1999, when Billy Davies could not find a regular spot for him in the first team, joining the Pars in the First Division for the millennium campaign.

Appearances 71 Goals 5

David MEIKLE

Meikle arrived at Fir Park in 1978 from Rancel Amateurs. David, a midfielder, made his debut in a goal-less draw at Partick in March 1979. When Ally MacLeod failed to take Motherwell back to the Premier Division in 1980, there were many casualties. David Meikle was one of them, having made just 7 appearances for Motherwell.

Appearances 5/2 Goals 0

Jan MICHELS

A freedom-of-contract signing from Go Ahead Deventer, Jan was another of the clutch of Harri Kampman signings who struggled to impose himself, following the departure of the likeable Finn. A neat midfielder, he could spray the ball about with efficiency and looked quick enough to cope with the frenetic Scottish game.

Appearances 7/3 Goals 0

Peter MILLAR

Peter Millar was a local boy who supported Motherwell, before taking up the game professionally with Arbroath from whence he went to Dunfermline for £12,000. He came to Motherwell on a free transfer in 1972. A strong, tireless player, Peter's best asset was his versatility and at Fir Park he served at full-back, central defence, midfield and attack – even playing wide on the wing! He gave great service and was often the unsung hero when

Peter Millar

others got the plaudits. He followed Stewart McLaren to Dundee in 1979.

Appearances 165/14 Goals 17

Greg MILLER

Released by Hibernian when they were relegated in 1998, Greg joined Motherwell, and sporadically showed up quite well. However, he was not quite up to scratch and was allowed to join Partick Thistle in the wake of Harri Kampman's departure from the hot-seat.

Appearances 1/3 Goals 0

Jimmy MILLER

Miller began his senior football with Aberdeen, before moving to Queen of the South in 1974. A chunky midfielder, Jimmy was a solid performer but an unspectacular one. This perhaps worked against him at Motherwell, where he was underestimated. He moved to Morton for £10,000 in 1978, where he won a First Division Championship medal and gave sterling service to the Cappielow idol Andy Ritchie. Ritchie had the genius but Millar was the kind of 'grafter' every midfield needs.

Appearances 35/2 Goals 1

Thomas MILLIGAN

Despite showing great promise as a junior with Lesmahagow, Tommy was able to manage just a solitary outing as a senior at Motherwell. Signed in 1961, his only game came in the 1961/62 season, against Airdrie at Broomfield. The fact that Motherwell lost 1-2 probably did not enhance his chances. He was given a free transfer in 1963.

Appearances 1 Goals 0

Paul MILLS

Mills was a forward who made one particular appearance for Motherwell with maximum effect. Coming on as substitute late in the game against

Angus Moffat

Dunfermline at East End Park on 26 September 1981, Paul scored with the last kick of the game and Motherwell won 2-1. The remainder of his Claret and Amber moments were not quite so spectacular and he drifted from the scene without ever really establishing himself. He was signed in 1980 from West Bromwich Albion and released one year later.

Appearances 1/8 Goals 1

Angus MOFFAT

Signed as a homesick seventeen-year-old from Southampton, Moffat made his debut in the 1965/66 campaign against Hibernian at Easter Road. He soon settled in as a lithe, tricky winger and netted his first goal in a 4-1 win over St Mirren in December 1965.

It was during the following season that he etched his name in Scottish Football history. The 1966/67 season allowed substitutes for the first time and Angus was named as twelfth man for the opening League Cup tie at Dunfermline. In a 1-2 defeat he came on as a second-half replacement and promptly scored, thus being not only Motherwell's first sub but their first scoring one too. He went on to establish himself that season and was an able supplier to 'Dixie' Deans and Bobby Campbell. Nevertheless, his stay with the club was to prove short. In 1968 he was sold to Detroit Cougars, as football enjoyed a brief boom in North America. It could well be that the strain of travelling to and from Helensburgh for club duties was a contributory factor to his low-key career at Fir Park.

Appearances 41 Goals 6

John MOORE

Although signed as a centre forward, none of John's three games for Motherwell came in the number 9 jersey. He wore the number 6 jersey in defeats by Aberdeen and Rangers and played his last game as a number 2 in a 0-2 reversal to Hibernian in March 1965. Signed in 1962 from North Motherwell, John was given a free transfer to Luton Town in May 1965.

Appearances 3 Goals 0

Ian MUIR

With the classy Willie Redpath as Motherwell's regular number 6, Ian had to look to other positions in which to deputise. He made three appearances at left-back and four at centre half. Born in Coatbridge, Ian stood at six feet tall and was an imposing left half. He joined the club from Thorniewood United in 1950.

Appearances 7 Goals 0

Jim MUIR

Muir was signed as a nineteen-year-old from Irvine Vics in 1967, on the same night as Joe Wark. Jim was a powerful player who cost the club just £250 and went by the delightful name of 'Jumbo' – which gave some idea of his size! He made his debut in 1968 in a 1-2 defeat by Hibs at Easter Road, and initially played as an outside-right before moving to the inside berth. He was always a 'trier' and consequently very popular with the fans on the terraces.

It was Jumbo who scored the goal against Morton in the League Cup quarter-final play-off that took Motherwell to the 1969 League Cup semi-final stage. Gradually he evolved into a centre forward, and his physique was ideal for this competitive role. However, the arrival of Ian St John as manager in 1973 saw Jim converted into

Jim Muir

a centre half, and he enjoyed a brief spell there before leaving the club. He had been seriously troubled by a groin injury in the spring of 1974 and this could well have been a contributory factor to his release.

He was sold to Alex Wright's Dumbarton on 26 August 1974. At Boghead he proved as much a cult figure as he had been at Fir Park. In his debut he gave a typically rumbustious performance in a 2-0 win over Clyde, as he settled down to defensive duties. He played alongside the McAdam brothers (Tom and Colin) at Dumbarton, both of whom would later star for Motherwell.

Appearances 129 Goals 31

John MUIR

Picked up on a free transfer from Rotherham United in June 1969, John was comfortable anywhere in the back line. Tough and reliable, he was with the club for a few seasons and, although never a flashy performer, was capable of making a big impact. He had the distinction of being signed for Rotherham by the legendary Tommy Docherty. John left Motherwell to join Stranraer in 1974.

Appearances 74/5 Goals 8

Frank MULVANEY

A young midfielder/winger who joined Motherwell from Forth Wanderers in 1985, Mulvaney was unable to take his opportunity in the Premier League. He made his debut at Ibrox in December 1985, Motherwell losing 0-1.

Appearances 4/1 Goals 0

Steve MUNGALL

Signed from Chapelhall in 1976, Steve made his debut at the tail end of the 1976/77 season. He was just beginning to show promise when he was sold to Tranmere Rovers in July 1979 and he

John Muir

went on to carve out a quite remarkably lengthy career on Merseyside.

Appearances 11/6 Goals 0

Jim MURPHY

When it became clear in 1969 that George Murray would be leaving the club, the search was on for another incisive and creative player. The search took Motherwell to Notts County, where the former Hearts and Raith Rovers winger Jim Murphy was plying his trade. Murphy made a great debut in the Second Division, scoring in a 3-1 win at Berwick Rangers. But it was his only goal of the season, as Motherwell pummelled the opposition week in week out on their way to the title. Back in the First Division he was a fringe player, but must have taken pride in scoring against his former employers at Raith.

Appearances 19/8 Goals 4

Steve Mungall

Derek Murray

Cammy MURRAY

A Kirkfieldbank market gardener, Murray usually operated at right-back for St Mirren. However, he was latterly a sweeper, a position in which he initially played for Motherwell reserves, before playing midfield for the senior team. Cameron, to give him his Sunday name, spent ten years with St Mirren before he joined Motherwell in the summer of 1972. Clearly he was more comfortable as a Buddie than a Steelman, for he only stayed at Fir Park for a single season. Cammy scored his only goal for the club in a 2-2 draw at St Johnstone. He then joined Arbroath, where his ability to play at either full-back or in midfield came in handy.

Appearances 7/2 Goals 1

Derek MURRAY

An understudy to Maurice Malpas at Dundee United, Derek jumped at the

George Murray

chance to join Motherwell in 1984. His transfer cost £8,000 and he was a very consistent performer, who in six years gave a string of very composed displays at left-back. Joining when Motherwell were in the First Division, he played in all but five matches as they romped to the title. He was to make a total of 95 League outings for The Steelmen before returning to his native Fife in 1988 with Raith Rovers. He spent two seasons as the regular left-back at Stark's Park before reverting to the junior ranks.

Appearances 93/2 Goals 0

George MURRAY

Elder brother of the aforementioned Cammy, George was signed by Bobby Ancell from Kilmarnock Amateurs in 1960. He stayed for seven years until the lure of Aberdeen proved too much. While at Motherwell he was capped by Scotland Under-23s against France, a game the young Scots won 3-0.

He made his debut at inside left in a no-score draw with Dunfermline at Fir Park, in March 1963, and had five League appearances that term before becoming a first team regular in the following season of 1963/64. His blond hair reminded many of the legendary Charlie Aitken. His move to Aberdeen saw Jimmy Wilson move to Fir Park in part-exchange.

Appearances 123 Goals 17

John MURRAY

An outside-left, John broke into the Motherwell side during the 1967/68 season. He made his debut in a 2-1 win at Stirling Albion in February 1968 and scored a few weeks later against Hearts at Tynecastle. A regular the following season, he dropped out of the Fir Park scene in the summer of 1969

Appearances 21/3Goals 3

N

Maxwell NELSON

An outside-left, Maxwell played just one game in Motherwell's colours, a 0-0 draw away to Falkirk in November 1955. The left-wing berth, for which he was initially signed, was at that point the property of Johnny Aitkenhead. When Aitkenhead

perhaps natural that Craig's own senior career should begin at Easter Road. He was a Scotland Under-21 international when Rangers signed him. A League Cup winner at Ibrox, he moved to Motherwell for £20,000 in 1986. Excellent in the air and a sound reader of the game, he gave Tommy McLean's side a very necessary solidity at the back and his partnership with Tom McAdam was a defensive cornerstone at Fir Park. A Scottish Cup winner at Motherwell, he eventually fell foul of Tommy McLean and was sold to Kilmarnock for £50,000 in October 1991. He thrived at Rugby Park.

Appearances 154/4 Goals 8

Andy PATON

Signed in 1942 from Kello Rovers, Andy Paton went on to become one of Motherwell's most popular post-war players. A commanding centre half, his game hinged on superb tackling and almost clairvoyant interceptions. He could dribble out of defence with great style and although this cost the club a couple of goals it provided sterling entertainment for well over a decade. Andy was at the heart of the Motherwell teams which won the League Cup and Scottish Cup in 1950 and 1952 respectively and he also picked up 3 Scotland caps. All in all, his was a marvellously distinguished career.

Although he joined Motherwell as a nineteen-year-old, he was already highly experienced, having made his debut for Irvine Meadow as a mere fourteen-year-old! Such prodigious progress was not too surprising, as he came from an established footballing family, an uncle had played with Motherwell, another with Newcastle United, yet another for Portsmouth, and Paton's father starred as an inside right with St Mirren, Derby County, Tottenham, Swansea and Watford.

It would be fair to say that indiscipline blighted Andy's early career at Fir Park and he was a frequent guest of the SFA. In one notable incident he was head-butted by an irate Partick Thistle player and many reporters would refer to 'the expressive arms of Andy Paton being thrown aloft'. One consequence of the Partick incident in 1947 was that Paton rarely shook hands after a match lest the same fate should befall him.

Once he had put his youthful impetuosity behind him, he matured into one of Scotland's outstanding defenders. In the season of 1950/51, he shackled the dangerous Lawrie Reilly to help Motherwell win the League Cup 3-0 against Hibs; indeed, he was Motherwell's captain on that dramatic afternoon, as he was later in the season

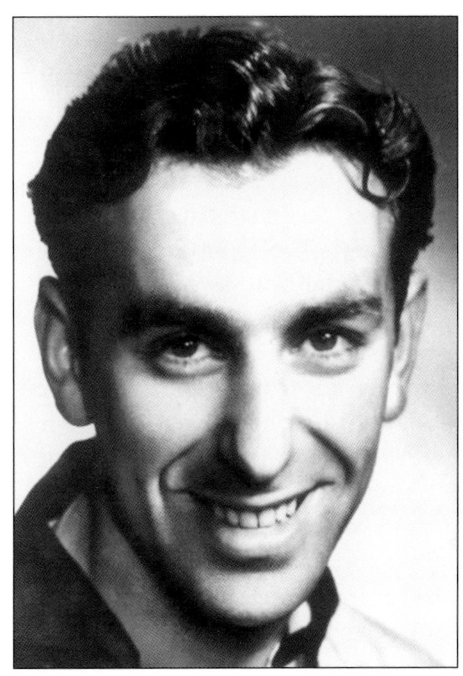

Andy Paton

when Motherwell also lost the Scottish Cup final. One year later he thwarted the brilliant Willie Bauld of Hearts as Motherwell advanced to a Scottish Cup final against Dundee. Earlier in the tournament he had set up the winning goal in a thrilling replay win over Rangers, after a famous meandering dribble upfield. It took Motherwell ten matches to land the elusive national cup!

Never a great goalscorer, he did notch up a handful, including a precious one against Rangers during a 3-3 draw in the 1952 League Cup competition. Indeed, as a youngster he scored three in one game for Kello – as an inside forward – and the Partick Thistle scout who was watching tried to sign him. In Andy's debut against Albion Rovers in December 1942 he was played as a centre forward, with none other than Jock Stein as his immediate opponent. Paton must have had the striker's knack, as he scored, but stopping goals was his forte and thence came his Scotland caps. Collected against Sweden, Denmark and Belgium, they went neatly with his war-time awards for playing against Wales and Ireland.

He was the first player to win the Motherwell FC Supporters' Association Player of the Year award. This was a fitting tribute to a man who would perhaps frustrate a manager but enthral supporters. Opposition supporters would bait him mercilessly, while Motherwell fans viewed him in an almost reverential light.

Andy was 'gifted' a free transfer in the summer of 1958, and after a year of playing became Hamilton Accies' boss in August 1959, presiding over one of their most successful spells. In 1965 he steered the club to the top flight, and when he left the club in 1967 he could reflect upon a lasting and rewarding spell at Douglas Park. Amongst his first signings for the Accies had been ex-Motherwell favourite, Wilson Humphries; another capture was Jim McLean, later to manage Dundee United with such distinction.

Appearances 301 Goals 1

Willie PATON

Paton always struggled in the wake of McLeod, Redpath, and Cox, who were fellow wing-halves at Fir Park. Nevertheless, Willie was a fine player who might have done better elsewhere. He was signed in 1947 from Bo'ness United and released in 1952.

Appearances 11 Goals 1

Willie PETTIGREW

A gifted striker, Willie was a natural goalscorer who relied on pace and speed of thought for the bulk of his goals. Rejected as a youngster by Hibernian, he flourished in the junior ranks with East Kilbride Thistle and thereafter was an instant hit in Motherwell's reserve side, bursting on to the first team scene in 1973 amid a welter of goals. He served the club for six years and there was great disappointment, but a degree of acceptance, when he elected to try his luck in pastures new during 1979.

Signed in 1973, he made his Motherwell debut in 1974, coming on as a substitute against St Johnstone on 27 October. A couple of weeks later he played against Hibs, but his breakthrough came at the end of the season, when he scored against Morton and followed up with strikes at the expense of Dumbarton and Falkirk.

Soon afterwards, a telepathic partnership was formed with former Liverpool star Bobby Graham, and Willie was a regular by January 1975. He scored 20 goals in 1974/75, including four against Ayr in a 5-1 romp and seventeen in a marvellous eleven-game spell. Second only to Kenny Dalglish in the Premier League scoring charts of 1975/76, he was out on his own during the next term, with 21 goals. He played in sides which reached semi-finals in the Scottish and Texaco Cups and was frustrated by a lack of honours when he left. Never short of speed or effort, he played his last game in May 1979 against Rangers before joining Dundee United in August 1979 for £100,000.

Following a brief spell in the Under-21 side, he had earned the first of his full international honours on 7 April 1976, when he made a scoring debut for Scotland in a 1-0 win over Switzerland. He scored in his next outing too, a 3-1 win over Wales. He picked up further caps against Northern Ireland, Wales and Sweden but could consider himself unlucky to win just 5 Scotland full caps.

Although discarded by the full side, a sign of Willie's reputation came in April 1978 when he played for the Scottish League against Italy 'B' in Verona. On Wednesday 1 November 1978, he received a second League cap when he played against the Irish League, at Fir Park no less. Scotland drew 1-1 and Willie capped a memorable night for Lanarkshire by netting Scotland's goal.

His stay on Tayside proved successful. In his first season there he scored 14 League goals, four in a dramatic 5-1 Scottish Cup win over Dundee and twice in the League Cup final as

Willie Pettigrew

United won their first ever piece of silverware. He collected another League Cup winners' medal the next season against Dundee. He also served Hearts, Morton and Hamilton Accies in a career which brought goals galore and great enjoyment to many.

Appearances 157/9 Goals 80

John PHILLIBEN

A very popular defender, John was a whole-hearted performer whose sheer professionalism always shone through. Never was this more abundantly displayed than after the 1991 Scottish Cup final. John had starred in several matches en route to the Hampden final, yet on the big day Tommy McLean elected to make Colin O'Neill a substitute at the expense of John. Given that O'Neill was glaringly unfit (he took to the field heavily strapped), this was a harsh blow for John, but he stayed

John Philliben

despite the snub.

Amongst his highlights for Motherwell were three outstanding goals. At Cappielow Park, Greenock he scored with a 'howitzer' of a 30-yarder, at Dundee United he scored a last minute equaliser in a pulsating Scottish Cup tie and at Fir Park he netted one of Motherwell's goals in a 3-0 win over Rangers just weeks before the 1991 Scottish Cup final. He left after a thoroughly merited testimonial, against West Ham United in 1998, and joined Stirling Albion, where he became manager. However, he continued his links with Motherwell, coming back time and again to recruit players and even selling the embryonic talent of Stephen Nicholas to Billy Davies. John had been one of Tommy McLean's first buys, being snapped up in September 1986 for £20,000 from Doncaster Rovers.

Appearances 302 Goals 7

Stewart POLLOK

A Bellshill lad, Pollok started with Glenafton Juniors, before going senior with Partick Thistle as an inside forward. National Service then interrupted his career and when it was over he was freed by Thistle. He was taken on trial by Bobby Ancell in December 1955 before being signed fully. During the 1955/56 season, Johnny Aitkenhead missed several matches and a string of players tried to fill the number 11 jersey. Pollok managed two outings (against Stirling Albion and Hibernian) but he, like Nelson, Williams and Rea, could not quite make a permanent stake to the outside-left position. Stewart was freed at the end of the season.

Appearances 2 Goals 0

Ian PURDIE

Although born in Motherwell in 1953, it was not until 1977 that Ian Purdie joined Motherwell, signing from Dundee. A slight and slender player, with a lethal left foot, he relied more on technique than brawn for his goals. Playing at number eleven, he was rarely absent in the first half of the 1977/78 campaign and scored against Partick, Ayr and Dundee United. He moved to Wigan after only a dozen or so Motherwell outings, and scored 12 times in 55 matches for them before making a move to Portsmouth. His career ended in 1979.

Appearances 11/5 Goals 3

Pat QUINN

Arguably the conductor of the 'Ancell Babes' midfield, Pat was a genuinely gifted player who relied on an astute football brain as opposed to speed or strength. His 'vision' and pin-point passing made him arguably one of the most gifted inside forwards of his era.

A career that was to lead to international recognition started with Bridgeton Waverely. In December 1955 Motherwell signed him and he made his debut in unusual circumstances, being a substitute for a friendly with Preston North End to mark the opening of Motherwell's floodlighting. Confident and charismatic, Quinn soon became a valuable link in the 'Ancell Babes' team.

There were many highs in his Fir Park career. He scored four times in the 9-1 hammering of Falkirk in a League Cup tie (Motherwell led an astonishing 9-0 at half time), three times in the 7-0 thrashing of Leeds United in a friendly and he played a key role in

Pat Quinn

the momentous 5-2 Scottish Cup win at Rangers. Capped 4 times by Scotland, and 6 times by the Scottish League, he made his debut in the 9-3 debacle against England at Wembley in 1961.

Alas, in November 1962 he moved to England and he scored on his Blackpool debut, a 3-1 win over fierce rivals Bolton Wanderers. A year later he joined Walter Galbraith's Hibernian side and after his Edinburgh playing days ended moved to East Fife as player/assistant manager before taking up coaching roles with Partick Thistle, Hibs, Motherwell and Hamilton.

Pat will always be remembered at Fir Park as a penalty-kick expert. Such was his ability and marvellous first touch that he always seemed to have ample time to deliver the telling pass. He would surely have prospered in the great Motherwell side of the 1930s.

Appearances 196 Goals 83

R

Stuart RAFFERTY

A powerful midfielder who knew the route to goal, Stuart gave Motherwell five years of excellent service and was part of Davie Hay's side that won the First Division championship.

He was signed as a seventeen-year-old from Port Glasgow Juniors by the inimitable Ally MacLeod. His debut came in the 1978/79 season and the former Scotland Youth cap gradually settled.

Stuart Rafferty

In the promotion campaign of 1982 he scored 7 First Division goals. The League was won in a canter, with Motherwell a full ten points ahead of second-placed Kilmarnock at the day of reckoning.

In 1984 he moved to Dundee, then managed by Archie Knox, and scored in his debut. He was to make 180 League outings for the Dark Blues and played in a Scottish Cup semi-final before moving to newly-promoted Dunfermline. In June 1991 he joined Morton and when his playing days ended he joined the Morton coaching staff.

Appearances 71/18 Goals 17

Dougie RAMSAY

A promising young reserve in the late 1990s, Dougie got his chance in the second half of the 1998/99 season. These outings were restricted to substitute appearances, but he did rather well and brought the curtain down on the season with a goal in Motherwell's 2-1 win at Dunfermline on the final day of the season. In the 1999/2000 season he found openings limited and made just two substitute appearances late in the campaign.

Appearances 0/6 Goals 1

Robert RAMSAY

Recruited from that useful training ground of North Motherwell Athletic, Robert had an immediate outing in the Lanarkshire Cup and made his debut against Falkirk at Brockville in November 1962. With players like Aitken and McCann dominating wing-half play, he had very little opportunity to progress. He joined Airdrie in 1965.

Appearances 5 Goals 0

Wallace REA

A native of Uddingston, he started with Larkhall Royal Albert and joined Third Lanark as an amateur in 1954. A year later he signed professional terms with Motherwell. At one time it looked as if Wallace might be the perfect replacement for Johnny Aitkenhead. In his second League game he scored against East Fife in a 2-0 win. He was only twenty at the time and lined up with Billy Reid (seventeen), Alex Bain (nineteen) and Archie Kerr (twenty) in a remarkably young forward line. But youthful enthusiasm could not grind out results and Wallace eventually left for England and Bradford City in 1959, having failed to fulfil the high expectations.

Appearances 14 Goals 3

Willie REDPATH

A cultured and creative player, Redpath won an impressive list of honours and was a considerable draw at the gate when in his prime. He earned a big reputation as a war-time footballer, and even appeared on stage with the *Sunday Mail*'s 'Rex' as a ball-juggler. When he arrived at Fir Park he quickly supplemented his income by betting fellow players that he could do two laps of the Fir Park playing pitch while playing continuous 'keepy-up'.

In a settled side, Redpath was a key player. During the successful Scottish Cup run of 1952 he scored both in the final and the decisive second semi-final replay. He was an elegant performer who created chances for others and could defend with equal effectiveness.

He enjoyed an excellent international career and was looked upon as something of a lucky mascot. In 1948 he made his Scottish League debut at Newcastle, in a 1-1 draw with the

Willie Redpath

Football League. Six games later he still hadn't tasted defeat and played in an 8-1 win over the Irish League. His full international debut came at Wales on 23 October 1948 and again he enjoyed the first six of his nine full caps without being on the losing side. Signed in 1946 from Polkemmet, he eventually joined Third Lanark in 1956.

Appearances 226 Goals 20

Billy REID

A schoolboy and youth international, Billy disappointed fifteen top Scottish and English clubs by signing for Motherwell in January 1955. But it was only natural that he should join his home town club, as his uncle was Tommy McKenzie, the former Motherwell wing-half, who was on the ground staff at the time.

A bustling, enthusiastic player, he made his debut against Dundee in March 1955 but, after much early promise, his career was eclipsed by the sparkling performances of Pat Quinn, Willie Hunter and his younger brother, Sammy. He was at Fir Park at a most competitive time. He joined Airdrie for £4,500 in October 1961. Billy will always be remembered at Fir Park for his titanic clash with 'Hard Man' Bobby Shearer when they both went for a 50-50 ball. Neither drew back an inch and the ball burst, with Bobby Shearer going right up in the air and over the top of the rock solid Billy before coming to rest, gasping for breath, flat on his back behind Billy. The referee gave an old

Joe Reid

fashioned 'stoat-up' to restart the game after Shearer had recovered.

Appearances 56 Goals 8

Joe REID

It was Joe Reid's misfortune that the bulk of his Motherwell appearances fell in the war-time seasons, which strictly speaking are unofficial. Nevertheless, he must have been quite a finisher. Signed from Polkemmet Juniors in 1941, he had only been at Fir Park a few months when he scored in both 2-1 victories over Celtic in the two-legged Summer Cup quarter-final. He scored 16 times in the 1942/43 season, but played in only a handful of games after the war before moving on.

Appearances 4 Goals 0

Sammy REID

A cunning and determined inside forward, Sammy made up for any lack of inches with a huge heart and a wonderful range of skills. That he was once signed by the legendary Bill Shankly was sufficient proof of his quality.

Sammy and his elder brother, Billy, were brought up in Craigneuk and were gifted young players. It was no surprise that both brothers were snapped up by The Steelmen. Billy went to Fir Park first and in due course Sammy followed. A Scotland schoolboy cap, he was also capped at Youth international level and had played alongside Joe Baker and Denis Law at schoolboy level.

Versatility was Sammy's hallmark, being able to play on either wing or at half-back and inside forward. In essence he was several players rolled into one. He made his Motherwell debut in the keenly-contested local derby with Airdrie on New Year's Day 1957 and within months would be part of the 'Ancell Babes' side. That forward line – Hunter, Reid, St John, Quinn and Weir – brought great pleasure to football fans throughout the country, regardless of their persuasion. Indeed, such was the quality of this forward line that the players frequently changed position.

Sammy quickly built up a pile of memorable events at Fir Park. He was part of the Motherwell side that became the first to beat Rangers four times in a single season and played in the 7-0 destruction of Leeds United. This earned him a move to Liverpool, where a young Scottish manager by the name of Bill Shankly was cutting his teeth.

Then came a four year stint at Falkirk, which saw Sammy show a

Sammy Reid

maturity that was essential to the progress of the Bairns at this time. His Brockville career began in 1960/61, when he made his debut in a Division Two match against Montrose. He was to play in 33 games that term and returned the useful scoring total of 20 goals. This was sufficient to steer Falkirk to promotion and he played the remainder of his Falkirk football in the top League.

After Falkirk, where he scored 25 times in 70 League appearances, came spells with Clyde and Berwick Rangers. It was of course while with the latter that Sammy became a household name. In January 1967 the minnows of Berwick beat the mighty Glasgow Rangers 1-0 in a Scottish Cup tie and Sammy scored the goal.

Appearances 61 Goals 18

John REILLY

There was a time when it seemed as if the majority of Motherwell transfers were negotiated over the McLean family dinner table. When Tommy McLean was in charge at Fir Park and his elder brother Jim was at the helm at Dundee United, an extraordinary number of United players ended up joining Motherwell. John Reilly was a case in point. He had been a successful fringe player at Dundee United, playing eight times in their championship winning side, but never quite establishing himself week in week out. Thus, in 1985 he took the road south to Fir Park. In truth it seemed like a good move for Motherwell and in his very first season he scored 9 times in only 30 matches.

The next season the return was poorer and then in seasons of 1987/88 and 1988/89, John failed to make a single appearance, being ruled out through injury. It seemed his career had been prematurely ended.

John was released and then quite suddenly in 1992 emerged from his injury nightmare and declared himself fit. He signed for Dunfermline and spent two seasons there, but made only six outings before an Indian summer at East Fife, where he bagged 5 goals in only 9 matches. His career thereafter took him to the footballing outposts of Cowdenbeath, Arbroath and Forfar Athletic, which was quite a turnaround for a man who scored in the 1982/83 European Cup campaign that saw Dundee United reach the semi-finals. He quit as East Fife assistant manager in March 2000 to resume his career as a sports writer.

Appearances 42/14 Goals 12

John Reilly

Mark REILLY

From being a fringe player at Motherwell in the 1990s with only a handful of outings to his name, Mark went to Kilmarnock and promptly became a fixture in their side. A combative and clever midfielder, he revelled in the Rugby Park scene and not only scored some wonderful goals but picked up a Scotland 'B' international cap. The highlight of his stay at Rugby Park was surely winning a Scottish Cup medal in 1997. A brief stint at Reading in 1998 was ended by Mark's return to Kilmarnock.

Appearances 4 Goals 0

Stuart RENNIE

Stuart rates with the best post-war 'keepers at Fir Park. A civil servant during the day, he was a more than a capable goalkeeper, as his appearance record proves. He joined Falkirk in 1967 from Royston Boys' Club and soon had a Second Division championship medal to his name. When he lost his Falkirk place to Ally Donaldson he moved to Motherwell in October 1973, as part of the deal that took striker Kirkie Lawson in the opposite direction. An agile 'keeper, he dominated his area and was known for his reflex saves.

He was also exceptionally brave. On 6 November 1976, Motherwell were two down to Kilmarnock at Fir Park in torrential rain, the pitch resembling a paddy field. Stuart's face came in contact with a Kilmarnock boot, leaving him with an open cheek wound. Refusing to come off, he had it stitched at half time and went out to defy Kilmarnock in the second half. Sensationally, Motherwell came back to win 5-4 thanks to a Jimmy O'Rourke thirteen-minute hat-trick, but even Jimmy pointed to Stuart as the real hero.

Appearances 174 Goals 0

Stuart Rennie

Franz RESCH

Resch played 3 games at the start of the 1997/98 season after being signed by Alex McLeish. An Austrian, born in Vienna, he arrived at the same time as Mario Dorner and seemed set to make an impact. He had played for Rapid Vienna and owned 5 full international caps when joining Motherwell. His departure was not popular with the Motherwell supporters, who had seen much in his play to recommend him. He later played in England with Darlington.

Appearances 3 Goals 0

Andy RITCHIE

One of the all-time great players in the history of Morton, Andy came to Motherwell after many years' service to the Greenock club – arguably too many. While at Morton he had evolved into something of a legend, with his awesome free-kick ability and general swagger and marksmanship. A Scotland Under-21 international, he had started out at Celtic but his laid-back style, which often bordered on the lazy, had meant a move was almost inevitable. He flourished at Benny Rooney's Morton. Alas, he was not able to reproduce his Morton form at Motherwell but his arrival was nevertheless interesting. He joined Motherwell in July 1983 for just £30,000 and was freed in January 1984.

Appearances 6/2 Goals 1

Billy RITCHIE

The last line of defence in Rangers' all-conquering side in the early 1960s Ritchie had won a string of honours by the time he ended his thirteen-year stint at Ibrox and joined Partick Thistle in 1967. He was therefore very much in the veteran stages when he joined Motherwell in August 1970. He stayed for one year before being released, having helped Motherwell out of a minor goalkeeping crisis.

Appearances 13 Goals 0

Bobby Roberts

Innes RITCHIE

Signed from Bathgate Thistle, Innes spent a two-year apprenticeship at Fir Park before making his debut. A central defender, he made few Premier outings for the club largely because Chris McCart, Brian Martin and Mitchel Van Der Gaag barred his route. He finally moved on in January 1997, to Jimmy Bone's East Fife.

Appearances 11 Goals 0

Bobby ROBERTS

Born in 1941, Bobby came to Fir Park in 1959 from Edinburgh Norton, as had Willie Hunter two years earlier. He came with a big reputation as a goalscorer, having netted an amazing 93 goals in one season with the Norton side. Deceptively frail in appearance, Bobby quickly revealed surprising stamina and speed and graduated rapidly to the first team. Signed as an outside-left, he was used as a centre forward early in his Fir Park career, as seen when he deputised for Ian St John against Toulouse in the Anglo-Franco-Scottish Friendship trophy, scoring both goals in a hard-fought 2-0 victory.

He appeared in other forward positions before settling into a wing-half role. Bobby was a popular and influential player with Motherwell, who was voted Motherwell Player of the Year in 1962. He gained a Scottish League cap against the Irish League in 1963, having been capped at Under-23 level against Wales in 1962, before moving to Leicester City in 1963 for a fee in excess of £40,000, a substantial sum in those days. He played in the 1969 FA Cup final and enjoyed a lengthy career with Leicester. After his playing career finished, he managed

Colchester United then Wrexham, leading the former to promotion out of the Fourth Division.

Appearances 91 Goals 26

Charles ROBERTSON

In 1941 Charles was signed from Armadale and he proved to be a useful inside forward. A player of no mean ability, he was unfortunate to be competing with Jimmy Watson and Gordon Bremner for the inside berths. He was released in 1950 and it would be fair to say his career was ruined by the demands of war-time national service. At the end of the war he was stationed in Belgium and guested for Standard Liege, where he was known as 'Le Diable Rouge' due to his red hair and aggressive style.

Appearances 16 Goals 6

James ROBERTSON

An inside left, James was a nippy little player who joined the club in 1963 from Bath City. He stayed for two years before he emigrated to South Africa in 1965. His main contribution came in 1963/64, with 21 League appearances and 2 goals, linking well with the main strike force, Joe McBride.

Appearances 23 Goals 2

Gordon ROBINSON

A single outing in the season that saw Motherwell win the Scottish Cup for the first time was Gordon's sole contribution to the history of Motherwell. His ninety minutes of fame came against Aberdeen at Fir Park in December 1951, and an exciting match it was too, with Motherwell and Aberdeen sharing six goals. Listed as an inside forward, he was born in Chesterfield and joined Motherwell from Sheffield United. He had very little opportunity, as Motherwell had a settled side despite heading to relegation in 1953.

Appearances 1 Goals 0

Andy RODDIE

Alex McLeish's first signing, Andy came (predictably) from his former club Aberdeen for £100,000 in August 1994. Alas, for all his skill Andy never quite settled with Motherwell and ultimately was the victim of some fairly harsh crowd criticism. A delicate winger, he clearly had talent and was keen enough in his early days. However, bad luck dogged his early performances and gradually he failed to deliver, looking increasingly lost in the helter-skelter of the Premier League. He left, having failed to live up to his six-figure price tag, and tried his luck in Sweden.

He returned to Scotland and played briefly for St Mirren before moving on to Stranraer. Signed by former Hamilton player Billy McLaren, he then scored his first goal against former team-mate John Philliben's Stirling Albion side.

Appearances 55 Goals 0

Ian ROSS

Born in Broxburn in 1974, Ian made his debut in the 1994/95 season and gradually proved himself to be a versatile young player. Signed as a forward, he was played as a midfielder in the early part of his career but retained his sense of finishing on one memorable occasion. The game in question was against Celtic at Fir Park and Motherwell were forced to play Jamie Dolan in goals after Scott Howie had sustained a broken

Ian Ross

cheek-bone. In the final minute Motherwell executed the perfect breakaway and Ross converted a chance from close in. The game was won 2-1 and Ian Ross had etched his own special place in Motherwell history. Ian moved to St Mirren in the summer of 2000 as the Paisley side returned to the Premier Division.

Appearances 46 Goals 1

Brian RUANE

Brian was a young striker who played in the first home League game of the 1979/80 season as a substitute at Clydebank and then started seven days later against Arbroath. However, he never featured again and was released at the end of the season. He had been signed from Lesmahagow in 1979. His lasting claim to fame was arguably his engagement to 'Gregory's Girl'.

Appearances 1/1 Goals 0

John RUSSELL

Russell was a stocky, talented wing-half, who was a regular until Willie Redpath made his bow in 1946/47. After that he was always third choice behind Willie and Donald McLeod. Signed from Pollok Juniors in 1943, he moved to Kilmarnock for £1,500 in August 1950.

Appearances 39 Goals 1

Bobby RUSSELL (1)

One game dominates when you consider the career of Bobby Russell. On the opening day of the 1962/63 season, Motherwell entertained Falkirk in a League Cup tie. At half time Motherwell were winning 9-0 and Russell had scored five times (Pat Quinn had scored four). Clearly, keeping up that level of scoring was a tall order that Bobby could not match.

Bobby had arrived with a great reputation, having netted 37 goals for Darvel Juniors in 1961/62 (a haul that

John Russell

Bobby Russell (1)

included eleven in his last four games there). He did end up with a good scoring record at Motherwell, and had a hat-trick against Raith Rovers in a 5-2 win. What ultimately sounded the death-knell on his Fir Park career was the arrival of the scoring phenomenon that was Joe McBride.

Appearances 19 Goals 8

Bobby RUSSELL (2)

A wonderful midfield talent, Bobby came to Motherwell late in his career but still managed to make over 100 outings. He had tried his luck at Sunderland before playing junior football at Shettleston. From there Rangers snapped him up, and he went on to win all the honours in Jock Wallace's treble-winning side, earning fame for a wonderful goal in Eindhoven.

When Tommy McLean brought him to Motherwell, a few eyebrows were raised but he proved to be another shrewd purchase. Although slightly built, he was a sound player when in possession and far harder to dispossess than his frame suggested. Creative and forward thinking, he scored a wonderful solo effort for Motherwell against Rangers in a 1-0 win at Fir Park in October 1989 as Motherwell surged to the top of the Premier League. However, he was plagued by injury and eventually his infrequent outings for Motherwell signalled his departure.

Bobby went to Northern Ireland from Motherwell, playing at Coleraine, where former Motherwell team-mate Colin O'Neill was manager. He then joined Ayr United in January 1993 but lasted only until March, when his knee problems finally forced him to retire.

Appearances 131 Goals 15

Bobby Russell (2)

S

Howard SAMEROFF

Signed in 1980 from Kirkintilloch Rob Roy, Howard played just four games in goal for Motherwell in 1981/82, as Motherwell won promotion to the Premier League. He spent one match on loan with Hamilton Accies and then reverted to playing junior football, this time with Pollok Juniors. He won a Junior Cup winners' badge with Pollok, before spells with Johnstone Burgh and Yoker.

Appearances 4 Goals 0

James SEITH

Recruited from Hill of Beath during the 1962/63 season, James made a single outing. Motherwell had lost 1-7 at Kilmarnock the previous Saturday and thus made changes for the visit of Dundee United a few days later. The game ended in a drab 0-0 draw and that was the sum of Seith's Motherwell career. He was listed as a winger.

Appearances 1 Goals 0

Davie SHANKS

A defensive midfielder, Davie was at his best when asked to 'shadow' a player throughout the duration of a game. He did this most memorably against 'Butch' Wilkins when Motherwell beat the Rangers in 1989. Sadly, a section of the Fir Park faithful never quite took to Davie and he had to battle against the critics throughout his stay at Motherwell. Once an 'S' form with Airdrie, he started his senior career with Cowdenbeath before going to Clydebank in 1984. He stayed there until Motherwell bought him in 1988, but one year later he was off to Falkirk. His next port of call was Stirling Albion.

Appearances 8/3 Goals 0

Mark SHANKS

Mark was the son of the former Airdrie full-back and was signed by Willie McLean in 1977 from Blackburn Rovers. A quick, determined defender, he tackled hard and made 13 first team appearances in 1978/79. At the end of the season he moved to Ayr United to be paired with a young Steve Nicol, later of Liverpool and Scotland fame.

Released by Ayr at the end of the 1984/85 campaign, he went to Cyprus, where his former Ayr boss Willie McLean was managing.

Appearances 10/3 Goals 0

Rab SHANNON

Signed from Dunfermline in July 1993 for £85,000, Rab was a vastly experienced full-back who served Motherwell well in the latter years of his career. Capable of playing in midfield too, he was a player whom Tommy McLean had tracked for several years.

Raised in Bellshill, he joined Dundee from schools football and was a regular in their first team as a teenager. He added Scotland Under-21 caps to his youth awards. In 1991 he moved to Dunfermline but within months he was sampling relegation for the second time in his career.

With Motherwell he showed himself to be determined, industrious and

Davie Shanks

clever with the ball. Perhaps not the most spectacular of players, he was nevertheless a very reliable one.

In 1999 he joined East Fife, where former Motherwell team-mate Stevie Kirk was the manager, and when Kirk was dismissed he assumed the mantle himself.

Appearances 64/2 Goals 3

Rab Shannon

Archie SHAW

A legendary left-back who served the club as a player for over fourteen years, Shaw went on to become coach and finally groundsman. He was often compared to Ben Ellis, the great Motherwell left-back of the 1930s. This was the ultimate compliment, which was thoroughly deserved.

Born in Netherton, Archibald Hamilton Rammage Shaw, or 'Baldy' Shaw as he was affectionately known, joined the club in 1942 from nearby Wishaw Juniors and was as solid as his trade of bricklayer suggested. He was a regular in the side throughout the 1940s and 1950s and thus won both League and Scottish Cup winner's medals. He also gained Scottish League caps and he was a fearsome competitor in any side in which he played. So much so that when he stepped down in 1955, he was thrust into the reserves and became an excellent coach. He made a brief comeback in the first team in the season of 1957/58, before reverting to coaching. Thus his final Motherwell game came as late as 14 December 1957, when Motherwell defeated Aberdeen 4-1 at Fir Park.

With another Motherwell legend, Willie Kilmarnock, Archie formed a full-back partnership that lasted fourteen years, a record surely no other club can boast. They certainly knew all about the off-side trap, much to the frustration of opposing forwards.

Never a great goalscorer, he nevertheless netted his first goal for the club early in his career, in a match against Partick Thistle in 1942. He would not score again until a Scottish Cup tie in 1947 against East Fife. Sadly, dedicated one-club icons like 'Baldy' Shaw have become an endangered species in the modern game.

Appearances 313 Goals 1

Tony SHEPHERD

A 5 ft 9 in midfielder who was originally a product of Celtic BC, Shepherd was with the Bhoys for five years before leaving Scotland in 1988. Ironically, Motherwell tried unsuccessfully at the time to persuade him to move to Fir Park. However, after a spell with Carlisle United, Motherwell finally got their man in June 1991, for £50,000. A skilful midfielder, his contribution was that of a fringe player and he moved on having failed to make the expected impact.

From Motherwell he moved to Portadown, and then back to Scotland with Ayr United.

Appearances 3/7 Goals 0

Paul SHEPSTONE

Paul was one of Tommy McLean's little surprise signings that did not quite work out. Plucked from Blackburn Rovers in June 1992, it takes just the merest glance at the football reference books to see that Paul had been tipped for big things. Alas, he never made the Fir Park breakthrough that was hoped for and was gone within a season of arriving, moving to Wycombe Wanderers

Appearances 1 Goals 0

Archie Shaw

Eliphas Shivute

Eliphas SHIVUTE
The wonderful skills of Eliphas Shivute were at Fir Park all too briefly. A Namibian international, Shivute was an entertainer and a charismatic striker. Fleet of foot and extremely tricky, he was as unpredictable as he was skilled.

Born in 1974 in Olujonda, Namibia, he was signed in 1997 from Eleven Arrows FC of Namibia, but had experience of European football as he had played in the lower leagues in Germany some years earlier. His career rather fizzled out at Fir Park but he did leave Motherwell the memory of a delicious goal at a sunny Ibrox.
Appearances 12/12 Goals 3

Neil SIMPSON
If ever a player had to carry baggage around in his career, it was Neil Simpson. Prior to an incident at Pittodrie, he was known as a young midfielder battler who, together with Neale Cooper, had given Alex Ferguson's Aberdeen side of the 1980s enough strength to better both Rangers and Celtic. Simpson and Cooper were the creative muscle-men of the Aberdeen side that won the European Cup Winners Cup and feared no-one.

Then Simpson's career was turned upside down when he committed an awful tackle on young Rangers and Scotland star Ian Durrant. Durrant suffered cruciate ligament damage and was lost to the game for over a year. Simpson, for his part, was castigated,

Tommy Sloan

Neil Simpson

roundly condemned and his own career never recovered. After a stint at Newcastle, he came to Motherwell. His return to Scotland could hardly go unnoticed and his time with Motherwell was undistinguished, as if hampered by the past. He always gave his all, however, and was more creative than given credit for. Nevertheless, the Durrant incident could not be laid to rest and he returned to his native north-east to find employment in the Highland League.
Appearances 32/1 Goals 1

Andrew SINCLAIR
Like many before and after him, Sinclair suffered from the permanent Kilmarnock-Shaw full-back pairing. He was signed in 1942 from Armadale Thistle and left in 1950 on a free transfer.
Appearances 11 Goals 0

Tommy SLOAN
A goal-scoring winger, Tommy joined Motherwell from Hearts, along with Charlie Cox, on Boxing Day 1951. Within weeks he had made a huge impact, proving himself a most useful forward.

Clearly the highlight of Tommy's career was being part of the Scottish Cup winning side in 1952, although this was pushed closely by his 'B' Championship medal in 1954. When Hearts won the Scottish Cup in 1956, their very next game was at Fir Park. Motherwell won 1-0 and Tommy scored the only goal against his former employers. A fast, and direct, winger with an eye for goal, he joined Gloucester City in 1957.

Appearances 113 Goals 35

Joe SMITH

A Glasgow lad, Joe was taken north by Aberdeen boss Eddie Turnbull as a fifteen-year-old and 'farmed out' to Banks O'Dee, with whom he won Scottish Youth caps. From there he graduated to the Dons reserves and then the senior side, in which he served under managers Ally MacLeod, Billy McNeill and Alex Ferguson. Sidelined by a serious leg injury for much of the 1977/78 season, he was top of Ally MacLeod's wanted list when the inimitable manager arrived at Fir Park, duly following Ally for a reported fee of £40,000. Highly regarded by MacLeod as a 'classy playmaker from the deep, who can also fit into a back four role', Joe made his debut in a home 1-1 draw with Partick Thistle in December 1978 and proved to be a consistent performer over three seasons at Fir Park. He lost his place in the Motherwell side late in the 1980/81 campaign, in the face of stiff competition from Steve McLelland, Joe Carson and Graeme Forbes. Joe's elder brother, Jimmy, had preceded him to Aberdeen.

Appearances 55/2 Goals 0

Paul SMITH

Paul was one of those players with superb balance and a wonderfully instinctive sense of where the goals lay. This was to be reflected in his excellent scoring record at a number of clubs. He started his career with Dundee and then, in truly nomadic fashion, took his boots to a variety of clubs.

From Dundee it was a short journey over the road to Dundee United. Then came a very impressive stint at Raith Rovers, which in many eyes made his reputation. During the 1985/86 season he scored 21 League goals and forged a formidable partnership with Keith Wright. Motherwell, under the guidance

Paul Smith

of Tommy McLean were next to call upon his services and he was to experience the joy and pain of reaching cup semi-finals while with Motherwell.

From Motherwell, his travels next carried him to Dunfermline – he cost Jim Leishman £35,000 in 1988 – and from there to Falkirk. Ironically enough, he made his League bow against Motherwell in a 1-1 draw at Brockville. There was still time for a clutch of clubs – Dunfermline, Hearts, Ayr United and finally Berwick – to utilise his services. He later became manager of Berwick and in 2000 led them to promotion.

Appearances 70/8 Goals 13

Alan SNEDDON

A right-back, Alan started his career with Celtic and had the unenviable task of emulating the feats of Scotland full-back Danny McGrain. It was, however, at his next club, Hibernian, that he really made his mark.

Brought up in Larkhall, he had watched Motherwell and Hamilton as a boy and was known to have sympathies for the club. He joined Larkhall Thistle in the junior ranks and had several senior offers, including one from Motherwell, before plumping for Celtic in 1977. He won a Scottish Cup medal in the infamous 1980 'riot' cup final, but never really established himself at Parkhead. Bertie Auld took him to Hibernian for £60,000, where he became a fixture in the Edinburgh side.

After clocking up over 300 League outings for the Hibees, and enjoying a testimonial against Aston Villa, he joined Motherwell in July 1992. A neat and tidy player, he brought experience to his role but was seen more as a stop-gap replacement than a long-term solution. He later joined East Fife and played for several years with the Fife club in the lower leagues.

Appearances 16 Goals 0

William SNEDDON

Signed from Hurlford United in 1950, William spent two seasons at Fir Park without being able to break into a very settled side. He was a member of the elite band of one game, one goal men.

Appearances 1 Goals 1

James SOMMERVILLE

James arrived at Fir Park as a teenage striker in 1977 and made regular appearances for the reserves that season. The following campaign he made three outings in the senior side, playing up front alongside Willie Pettigrew. He made additional appearances on the bench, but outings became rarer and rarer. At the end of 1978/79 he was given a free transfer – yet another promising youngster who failed to make it at Fir Park.

Appearances 3 Goals 0

Gordon SOUTAR

A competitive midfielder, Gordon was brought to Fir Park by Ally MacLeod in 1979 from Falkirk and quickly settled into the senior side that term. Despite his 32 League appearances and 5 goals, mostly from the penalty spot, he was unable to savour promotion. This also eluded him during the following season, in which his 18 appearances brought 3 counters. Sadly, he was unable to win a first team spot, as Motherwell romped back to Premier football in 1981/82.

Appearances 52/3 Goals 8

John Spencer

John SPENCER

One of the most exciting of all Motherwell signings, John arrived early in the John Boyle era. He responded by scoring the only goal in his debut, which came against one of his former clubs, Rangers.

Small for a striker, John had strength and a shrewd footballing brain which served him well. He was confined for long spells to the Rangers reserve side, but a move to Lai Sun in Hong Kong sparked his career into life. He then moved very successfully to Chelsea before sampling life with QPR and Everton. With 14 Scotland caps, it was clear that he was a quality performer.

Interestingly, he was a brother-in-law of manager Billy Davies!

Appearances 49 Goals 18

Hugh SPROAT

Eccentricity is often associated, sometimes unfairly, with goalkeepers, but Hugh or 'Shuggie', as he was dubbed, was undoubtedly something of a strong personality. Signed from Ayr United in July 1979, Hugh was a showman who took to sporting outrageously coloured earrings which, together with his huge 'Zapata' moustache, made him rather distinctive.

Fortunately, he could play a bit as well and Ally MacLeod, who had been his boss for a spell at Ayr, had no doubts on this score. Neither did Davie Hay and Sproat was the regular goalkeeper as Motherwell raced to promotion in 1982. He returned to Ayr United in 1984 and took his total number of outings for Ayr to 189 before retiring. Away from football, he worked in an Ayr bakery.

Stories abound about Sproat. He loved occasional forays upfield and was exceptionally quick off his line. He liked to command his penalty area and attributed his rapidly greying hair to the

Hugh Sproat

defences he played behind. Above all, he was a character.

Nothing summed up the personality of Hugh Sproat more than the story of how he almost had an impact on the World Champions. On 16 September 1978, Ayr United had a home match with Dumbarton. That morning, milkman Hugh Sproat wrenched his back while lifting a crate. Reserve goalkeeper Richard Northcote, also injured, had to deputise and, through no fault of his own, had a nightmare of a match in a 2-5 defeat. Ayr manager Alex Stuart was already under pressure and this result generated further public ire which no doubt influenced his decision to resign before the next match. Ally MacLeod quit the Scotland job to return to Ayr United and Jock Stein left Leeds United to fill the vacancy left by Ally MacLeod. There was much speculation about who would take over the Leeds United job and one of the names mentioned by the media was Cesar Luis Menotti, manager of the reigning World Champions Argentina. It was a move which did not materialise and it was just as well – if the World Cup holders had lost their manager it would have been a development which had its origins in Hugh Sproat's milk round.

Football seems to be losing the characters like Hugh Sproat and that is a sad development.

Appearances 146 Goals 0

Ian St John

Ian St JOHN

The centre forward most people associate with the 'Ancell Babes', the Saint was a brilliant finisher who exploited the skills of Hunter, Quinn, Reid and Weir superbly. However, it should be noted that he was extremely skilled himself and prolific in the air for a forward of average height. It is often overlooked that he had only four seasons at Fir Park, so the impression he made in such a short time is all the more remarkable.

Born in Motherwell, he joined in 1957 after a brief stay with Douglas Water Thistle. In his trial for Douglas he had scored four times and he scored when representing the Lanarkshire Junior side against Glasgow Juniors. Once settled at Fir Park, he was a regular marksman. Ironically, he perhaps benefited more than most players from the advent of floodlighting at Fir Park, for he shone brightly in the glamour friendlies that punctuated his stay in Lanarkshire.

In 1958/59 he hit 31 goals and his scoring became legendary. The two-and-a-half-minute hat-trick away to Hibs in a League Cup tie, on 15 August 1959, earned him great fame, as did his six goals against Brazilian aces Flamengo. But it was his consistency that caught the eye. Following a couple of impressive games for the Under-21s, his first full international cap came against West Germany in 1959 and he quickly added others against Northern Ireland, Wales, England, Poland, Germany and Austria as well as a handful of Scottish League honours

In May 1961 he joined Liverpool for £37,500 (a sum which went some way towards funding the building of the new main stand at Fir Park) and was a huge success with the Merseysiders. In his debut – against Everton – he scored a hat-trick and thus won the instant approval of the Kop. He went on to increase his haul of international caps to 21 and won 2 League Championship badges and an FA Cup winners medal, scoring the winning goal in a thrilling 2-1 win over Don Revie's Leeds. He finished his career with short spells at Coventry and Tranmere and then returned to Motherwell to manage the club in June 1973.

His stay as boss was impressive. He rejuvenated the side and installed first Bobby Graham and then Willie Pettigrew in a side which regularly drew crowds in excess of 10,000. Had he not left for Portsmouth in September 1974 after just fifteen months at Fir Park, who knows to what heights he might have steered Motherwell. As it was, there was no consolation in his admission that going to Portsmouth 'was a huge mistake'.

His breakthrough into broadcasting came via Radio Merseyside and a commentators' competition. He reached his broadcasting peak in the hugely popular 'Saint and Greavsie' show, which he co-hosted with former England striker Jimmy Greaves, and he is now established as a major television pundit.

Appearances 113 Goals 80

Alan STENHOUSE

A very talented inside forward who was signed by Bobby Ancell from Edina Hearts in 1957, Stenhouse was most unfortunate to be at Fir Park when there was such a wealth of young gifted players. Freed at the end of the 1961/62 season, Alan had stayed a long time for his 5 games and 1 goal.

Appearances 5 Goals 1

Gregor STEVENS

How do you summarise the black and white career of Gregor Stevens? With Motherwell he was a fresh-faced and talented young defender capable of playing in midfield. He had skill and strength and a youthful desire to succeed. However, he is remembered for none of the above due to a chaotic spell with Rangers which degenerated into farce as he was sent off time after time after time, occasionally for wild tackles that became notorious.

It is best, perhaps, to dwell on his Motherwell career, which began in the mid-1970s and ran for just over 150 competitive matches. He was capped by Scotland at Under-21 level and left to join Jock Wallace at Leicester for £165,000 in 1979. Things did not work out in the Midlands for Gregor and John Greig signed him for Rangers within the year, this time with a £150,000 cheque. The rest, as they say, is history.

He later came back to Motherwell briefly, before joining Partick Thistle in November 1984.

Appearances 144/319

Morris STEVENSON

An Edinburgh lad, recruited from Cockenzie Star in 1960, Morris started his senior career with Motherwell and then joined Hibernian in 1962. However, after just a dozen games he was granted another free transfer, after only one season at Easter Road, and moved to Hal Stewart's Morton. The move to Morton proved the making of him and he became an integral part of the Stewart-inspired Morton side in the late 1960s.

Whether or not his departure from Motherwell was a wise move was debatable, as he had scored 3 times in his 12 matches and shown flashes of genuine skill. However, Walter Galbraith, the Hibs boss, was persistent and knew that Stevenson could forage and drive. Stevenson teamed up with former Motherwell striker Gerry Baker at Easter Road. As well as starring with Morton he also served Luton Town and Dundee United.

Appearances 12 Goals 3

Gregor Stevens

Rab Stewart

Rab STEWART

Signed from Dunfermline, Rab was the club's top scorer as they won promotion in 1984/85 with 9 goals. Capable of performing well out wide or through the middle, he was both fast and courageous. His 1984/85 performance was particularly good, as he was sidelined for some months with an ankle injury. He went to Falkirk in 1985, as a makeweight in the deal to bring Crawford Baptie to Fir Park.

Appearances 25/8 Goals 10

Jered STIRLING

Conveniently enough, Jered was born in Stirling. He joined Motherwell from Partick Thistle in 1998 as a goalscoring full-back, the bulk of his goals coming courtesy of a panache with free-kicks and a calmness from the penalty mark. He started well at Fir Park and got Motherwell

Hugh Strachan

off to a winning start in the 1998/99 campaign with the only goal against St Johnstone on day one. However, he fell from favour at Fir Park and was frozen out of the picture for several months before leaving. Prior to serving Partick, he had played junior football with Shettleston and St Rochs.

Appearances 4/1 Goals 1

Hugh STRACHAN

Signed from Cumnock Juniors in 1957, Hugh was a strong player but in six years at Fir Park was frustrated by the lack of first team openings. A native of Kilmarnock, he was unable to command a regular spot at Motherwell and moved on a free transfer to Morton in 1963. Hugh made himself thoroughly at home in Greenock and became a solid performer. He won two Second Division Championship medals with Morton, as well as a League Cup runners-up badge. Extremely versatile, he played as a centre forward, a centre half and as an inside forward.

Appearances 27 Goals 4

Greg STRONG

Signed from Bolton Wanderers as Motherwell desperately sought to shore up a defence weakened by the loss of Shaun Teale, Strong was, in essence, strong by name and strong in physique.

He immediately gave the Motherwell central defence solidity and it was probably his success as much as anything which allowed the club to release Greig Denham. Strong made his debut in a 0-0 draw at Tynecastle and settled fairly quickly. His signature from Bolton proved a little elusive and it took the club until the summer of 2000 to make the deal permanent.

Appearances 10 Goals 0

T

Ian TAYLOR

Taylor had one tremendous goal above all others to look back on. While an Aberdeen player in the 1967/68 season, he scored the goal that gave the Dons a 3-2 win at Ibrox on the last day of the season. That was the only game Rangers lost in the League all season and they lost the title to Celtic by virtue of just two points. A goal to remember in every sense of the phrase.

Slightly built, he had great pace and an excellent first touch. Sadly, he never showed the form with Motherwell which had marked him as an exceptional talent in his early days at Aberdeen. He came to Fir Park in 1974 and, given that he could play either wide on the left or in midfield, he was a useful acquisition. He left for St Johnstone in 1976.

Appearances 38/10 Goals 5

Shuan TEALE

A hugely experienced defender, Teale spent sixteen excellent months with Motherwell, organising the defence and proving an inspirational presence. Sadly his period at the club ended on a sour note when he fell out with chairman John Boyle and manager Billy Davies over a new contract.

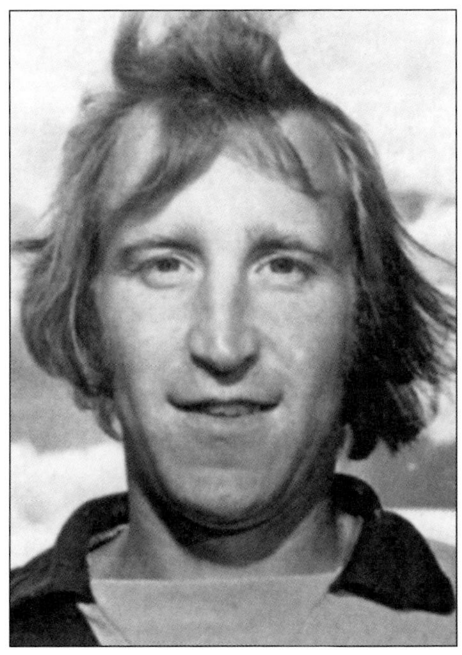

Ian Taylor

Shaun Teale

A late starter in football, he began in English non-League circles, serving Southport, Northwich Victoria and Weymouth before making his debut for Bournemouth at the less than tender age of twenty-four. His next move took him to Aston Villa, where he won a League Cup Winners badge and made over 150 outings. Tranmere took him next and then it was on to Hong Kong and Happy Valley. However, it was his stint at Tranmere that had acquainted him with Pat Nevin, John Boyle's right hand man.

At Fir Park he played with vigour and passion and was a huge favourite with the support. After Motherwell he played with English Third Division side Carlisle United.

Appearances 45 Goals 3

William TELFORD

A stocky bustling striker, also known as 'John', Telford was signed from Third Lanark in 1949 and made 7 appearances in 1949/50. He did not score, but three of the appearances were at left-half. That season he was top scorer with the reserves, with 12 goals. However, despite 13 goals for the reserves in the following season of 1950/51, he was placed on the open to transfer list. Prior to playing with Third Lanark, John was with St Mirren and after his stint at Fir Park served both Ayr United and Cheltenham United.

Appearances 7 Goals 0

Tony THOMAS

With former Everton and Tranmere winger Pat Nevin in place as chief executive, it was perhaps understandable that many of the early incoming transfers in the John Boyle reign were linked to the north-west of England. Tony Thomas had played with Nevin and was recruited as a defender.

Thomas had been with Tranmere for eight years and, remarkably, had already played at Wembley five times in various play-offs and cup-ties before moving to Everton. It was a big move that did not work out for him. When he came to Motherwell the club already had Ged Brannan, Shaun Teale and of course Pat Nevin on board, so the move should have been comfortable for him. However, he failed to settle into the first team and was very much a fringe player. Injuries hugely hindered his progress at Fir Park and in the 1999/2000 season he was ruled out from October onwards.

Appearances 16 Goals 0

Billy THOMSON

A 6 ft 3 in goalkeeper, Thomson was one of the best of his era. His career began with Partick Thistle in 1975 and he won 2 Under-21 caps while at Firhill, without ever making a first team outing for Partick. The reason he never reached the first team was simple – he was understudy to Scotland's Alan Rough. In 1978 he joined St Mirren and, while there, won 7 full Scotland caps and took his Under-21 haul to 8 caps. Dundee United bought him from St Mirren for £70,000 in June 1984 and he stayed with United until 1991, when Motherwell signed him for £50,000 in the wake of the fall-out with Ally Maxwell.

For three years he vied with Sieb

Billy Thomson

Dykstra for the first team jersey and whilst Dykstra was more flamboyant and noticeable, Thomson was dependable and highly experienced. If proof were needed of Thomson's ability it came in 1994, when Rangers stepped in and took him to Glasgow. His senior career ended at Dundee, where he ultimately coached Robert Douglas.

Appearances 52 Goals 0

Ian Thomson

Ian THOMSON

A forceful and strong inside forward, it is difficult to avoid the feeling that Ian Thomson should have got more from his Motherwell career. After all, his total of 13 League goals in only 55 starts bears comparison with most players filling this position.

Signed in 1962 from Musselburgh Windsor, he was freed in 1968.

Appearances 55 Goals 13

Matt THOMSON MBE

For nine years Matt Thomson was a regular in the Motherwell defence and there were few players more committed to victory. A member of the Summer Cup-winning side in 1965, he had been signed by Bobby Ancell and played alongside the likes of Hunter, Weir and Quinn.

Matt Thomson

A gifted junior international, Bobby Ancell had to beat several other clubs for Matt's signature. He made his debut in August 1961 and immediately became a first team regular. He was strong and resolute – someone even the most confident of forwards would not relish playing against.

When he retired from playing he built up his own printing business, to the extent that it became the largest printers in Scotland, and he was awarded the MBE. His achievement

Derek Townsley

therefore was to be a captain of Motherwell and a captain of industry – not a bad 'double'.
Appearances 172 Goals 0

Scott THOMSON
When Scott Howie departed for Reading, Motherwell needed backup for Stevie Woods. The answer came in the form of Scott Thomson, who came north from Hull City. However, he was remembered for a game in the colours of Raith Rovers, being the man who ensured they won the 1995 Scottish League Cup final against Celtic in a penalty shoot-out.
Appearances 1 Goals 0

James TONER
Formerly with Dundee and Leeds United, Bobby Ancell signed Toner early in the 1955/56 season on a free transfer. If you are to play only one League game for Motherwell then Celtic Park is as good a place as any to enjoy the ninety minutes. James played in a 2-2 draw at the start of the 1955/56 season. Other openings did not follow, however, and he moved to Forfar Athletic in 1956.
Appearances 1 Goals 0

Derek TOWNSLEY
Signed in the summer of 1999 from Queen of the South, Derek was an

unlikely looking winger, being 6 ft 5 in tall. His technique was deceptively relaxed, but he had a keen eye for goal and showed that early in his Motherwell career, with a splendid strike in the 3-2 victory over Celtic at Fir Park. He had played with Gretna in the Unibond League before he joined Queens.

Appearances 16/9 Goals 1

Paul TRACEY

Paul had three appearances as a substitute in 1983/84, but failed to make an impact. Although he featured in the reserves in 1984/85, he was clearly not in Tommy McLean's plans and was released.

Appearances 0/3 Goals 0

Kevin TWADDLE

A tall winger who was signed from Morton in the close season in 1999, he gave Motherwell a potent strength down the flanks, along with Derek Townsley. Unfortunately, Kevin was struck down almost immediately with glandular fever and the £120,000 signing had to wait until late September to make his full debut. However, his signing was an exciting one and he proved his worth in October of 1999 when he scored the only goal of the game as Motherwell won 1-0 at Celtic.

In the season prior to going to Fir Park he had hogged the headlines at Greenock Morton with his direct running and goalscoring prowess and this mirrored earlier spells with Raith Rovers and St Johnstone. Indeed, Kevin reportedly cost Rovers £82,000 when moving from Perth. Given his gangly appearance and knack for the unexpected, it seemed safe to assume he would prove very popular at Motherwell, despite being an avid Hearts fan!

Appearances 18/5 Goals 5

Simo VALAKARI

A Helsinki-born midfielder who joined Motherwell in 1997 from Finn PA, Valakari was more of a defensive midfielder than an attacking prospect. He added much needed industry to the Motherwell engine room. Not a player with flair and not the most aggressive of players,

Simo Valakari

Mitchel Van Der Gaag

he was nevertheless a dependable and whole-hearted performer whose consistency earned him a long stay in the first team. A Finnish Under-21 and full international, he continued his international ventures while at Fir Park and went on to become the most capped Motherwell player in history.

In the summer of 2000 Simo joined Derby County in a Bosman signing, meaning that Motherwell received no transfer fee. He left, perhaps at the peak of his career, aged twenty-seven, but remarkably without a single goal in his entire Fir Park career.

Appearances 104 Goals 0

Mitchel VAN DER GAAG

A classy Dutch defender, Mitchel was Motherwell's record signing at £400,000 and had a strange start to his career. He was only two games into his time at Fir Park when he was badly injured and this led to a long spell on the sidelines. However, he came back and left a lasting impression at the club. One key moment defined his Fir Park career. In the final match of the 1996/97 season Motherwell needed to take something from the game, an innocuous-looking home clash with already safe Dunfermline. It turned into a contest of high drama, with Dunfermline raising their game and at one stage leading 2-1. With eight minutes to go, relegation looked a distinct possibility but up stepped Van Der Gaag to thump home a sensational drive from some thirty yards. It was a wonderful strike and a saving one at that. What a way to bring down the curtain on your Motherwell career! Mitchel moved back to the Netherlands following the Dunfermline game.

Appearances 40 Goals 7

Bart VERHEUL

A Dutch striker who promised much, he was signed as a nineteen-year-old from Go Ahead Eagles by Tommy McLean. Sadly, young Bart was dogged by injury and failed to make the expected impression. Quick and alert, he made just four League outings and three of those were from the bench. He left having suffered a broken leg and having failed to carve out a regular place.

Appearances 1/3 Goals 0

W

Andy WALKER

A striker of lightning quick reflexes, young Andy Walker made quite an impression at Motherwell. Not only

Andy Walker

Nicky Walker

could he score goals but he could create them for those around him with his constant harrying of defenders and thoughtful use of the ball.

Powerful and direct, Andy Walker came to Fir Park via Ballieston Juniors and continued the tradition of outstanding Motherwell centre forwards. An extremely popular player with Motherwell fans, he scored the goal against Brechin which clinched promotion in May 1985. Sadly, like many Motherwell strikers before him (McBride, Deans and McClair) he was sold to Celtic before he had matured into the finished article. He was a sensation at Celtic, whom he joined for £350,000 in 1987, and at his next club, Bolton. Indeed he learned much from his spell in England with Bolton, where he scored 44 goals in 67 matches and had the good fortune to score a dramatic televised goal in the FA Cup for Bolton at Liverpool. From Bolton his travels took him over the Pennines to Sheffield United and then on to Hibs, Raith Rovers, Ayr United, Carlisle, Partick, Isernia of Italy and Alloa Athletic. He brought in the new millennium by joining Alloa Athletic as they chased and ultimately won promotion from the Second Division. After 3 goals in 8 games he retired to become a football agent and to continue writing his witty and perceptive Sunday newspaper column.

Appearances 85/11 Goals 17

Nicky WALKER

A graduate of Highland League football, Nicky played with Motherwell, Leicester City and Rangers and was one of Jock Wallace's favourite players. Clearly a sound prospect during his time at Fir Park, he was sold to Jock Wallace's Rangers in a deal which gave Motherwell Kenny Black and Kenny Lyall plus £100,000. With Wallace having been Motherwell boss shortly before his return to Rangers, such activity was widely predicted. From Rangers he moved to Hearts, in a deal that cost the Edinburgh club £125,000. Nicky ended his senior playing career back in the Highlands with Ross County when they joined the SFL and quickly won two promotions, firstly to the Second and then to the First Division.

Appearances 30 Goals 0

Billy WALLACE

A tall, strapping wing-half signed from

Lugar Boswell in 1962, Wallace scored on his Motherwell debut in a 4-1 win against Falkirk. He played a few weeks later in a 3-3 draw against Third Lanark but was given a free transfer at the end of the 1963/64 season.

Appearances 2 Goals 0

Joe WARK

Right up with the best in the Motherwell 'Hall of Fame', only Bobby Ferrier and George Stevenson played more times for Motherwell than the remarkable Joe Wark. Serving the club between 1968 and 1984, Joe was a left-back who established himself as a fixture in the Motherwell side. A classy performer, he was a tidy, creative player who was respected for his fair approach to the game.

Born in Glasgow in 1947, Joe was signed from Irvine Vics. He made his debut in a pre-season friendly in 1968 against Tranmere and it proved a bizarre occasion. Within three minutes 'keeper Keith MacRae was injured and Joe spent the remainder of the game in goal – he kept a clean sheet in a 2-0 win!

By a strange coincidence the same thing happened four years later, when he replaced the injured Billy Ritchie between the sticks and helped the club to another 2-0 win. But it was as a full-back that Joe made his name. Quick-tackling, athletic, and a perfect team-player, Wark was always amongst the first names pencilled into any Motherwell team.

He played for the club in Anglo-Scottish and Scottish Cup semi-final matches, but major honours eluded him. Most surprising of all, a full cap evaded his grasp, but in 1976 he did play for the Scottish League against their English counterparts.

In his first season at Fir Park, Joe played as an inside forward and scored 8 goals, including a hat-trick against Montrose, as the side romped to the Second Division title. That Championship badge was the first honour Joe collected in his Fir Park career.

In 1978 Joe was awarded a testimonial and West Bromwich Albion supplied the opposition. Amazingly, West Bromwich, inspired by Laurie Cunningham and Cyril Regis ran out 8-1 winners! If ever a player deserved two testimonials it was Joe Wark, and Motherwell tried again in January 1985 when a Motherwell All-Stars side lost narrowly to a Rangers-Celtic select.

Appearances 464/5 Goals 14

Bobby WATSON

A former Scotland schoolboy international, Bobby Watson was the proverbial

Joe Wark

powerhouse who could combine effective tackling and enthusiasm with good distribution. He began his career as an old-fashioned wing-half and, like so many thinking players, finished it as an orthodox defender. His six years at Fir Park as a player were memorable, so much so that he returned in November 1983 to manage the club for a short spell.

Signed by Rangers in 1963, he won a Scottish Cup winner's badge there in 1966. However, he was never an automatic choice and in 1970 joined Motherwell in a three-player deal that saw Bobby and Brian Heron come to Fir Park and Peter McCloy move to Ibrox. Manager Bobby Howitt soon made Watson his club captain and he responded by netting a memorable first goal for the club in a magical Texaco Cup win over the mighty Tottenham Hotspur. Bobby, who won a Scotland cap against the USSR in 1971, retired rather prematurely from playing in 1976 to concentrate on his steel stockholding business, but he was unable to keep away from football. He was a frequent attendee of Airdrie matches and was soon installed as boss at Broomfield. In 1983 he returned to Motherwell, this time as manager. However, it was not a good period in the club's history and he left in May 1984 as the club slipped to relegation.

Appearances 179/3 Goals 2

Jimmy Watson

Jimmy WATSON

Born in Plains, Lanarkshire, Jimmy Watson was a prolific marksman for Motherwell between 1943 and 1952. He netted the opening goal in the Scottish Cup final win over Dundee but left the club a few weeks later in controversial circumstances. However, he enjoyed a highly successful spell in England with Huddersfield before finishing his senior career with Dunfermline Athletic.

Watson scored Motherwell's goal in the 1945 Southern League Cup final, when Rangers pipped Motherwell 2-1, and he scored twice in the outstanding 4-1 win over Celtic in a League Cup quarter-final. Indeed, he was something of a cup expert, as his games to goals ratio proves – Scottish Cup 51 games:21 goals, League Cup 26:10, Summer Cup 6:7. His partnership with men like Archie Kelly and Jim Forrest made Motherwell a high-scoring side. Jimmy caught the international selectors' eye too, being capped in 1947 against Northern Ireland, and he would add another cap when he joined Huddersfield (again versus Northern Ireland).

Willie Watson

His departure from Fir Park was a sorry episode which owed more to money than any footballing shortcomings. He joined Huddersfield, then managed by Scot Andy Beattie, in June 1952 for £10,250. His place in the West Yorkshire side was secure until the arrival of Denis Law. Jimmy played 140 games for Huddersfield and scored 29 goals, but despite that he was sold to Dunfermline for just £1,250.

He spent three years with the Pars and the highlight of that stay surely had to be playing in the famous 10-1 win over Partick Thistle, a result that ensured Dunfermline stayed up in the 1958/59 season. Somewhat ironically, Jimmy did not score in that avalanche!

Appearances 195 Goals 66

Willie WATSON

Willie was signed in 1973 from Manchester United on a free transfer. He had spent eight years at Old Trafford, making 25 first team appearances. A robust defender whose experience gave him great positional sense, he gave Motherwell good service until he left in 1978. He had been a much sought-after teenager, winning no fewer than 15 Scottish schoolboy caps before being attracted by the lure of Manchester United. It was fitting that he made his debut at Celtic Park in the League Cup, with Motherwell achieving their first competitive win over Celtic in over four years. This proved to be the springboard for a sound career with The Steelmen.

Appearances 71/2 Goals 2

Willie WATTERS

Watters was a clever, direct right-winger, who on signing from Bonnyrigg Athletic in 1947 made an immediate impact, missing only two League games in 1947/48. But fortunes can

Willie Watters

Andy Weir

change very quickly in football and Willie had but one appearance the following season, Ian Goodall being preferred for the outside-right berth. To his great credit, Willie fought his way back into the side with some notable performances and did well in the next two seasons. The highlight of his career was in the League Cup final of 1950/51, when he scored a goal in Motherwell's 3-0 victory over much-fancied Hibs. That season he missed out on a Scottish Cup final appearance as Motherwell fell 0-1 to Celtic, with Wilson Humphries being given the number seven shirt. After four seasons at Fir Park, where he had been very popular, Willie refused to re-sign for 1951/52, requesting a transfer. He moved on to Dunfermline a few months later.

Appearances 61 Goals 7

Andy WEIR

Signed from Arthurlie in 1957, Andy was an orthodox left-winger. His speed and trickery made him a feared opponent, and were it not for a series of appalling injuries he would surely have achieved even greater fame in the game. As it was Andy gained 6 full Scotland caps, 3 Under-21 awards and a single Scottish League cap.

He won his first Scotland cap in 1959, in a team that contained three Motherwell players: Weir, Ian St John and Bert McCann. Given that Andy had followed the wonderful Hibernian winger Willie Ormond into the number 11 jersey, he was clearly highly regarded.

Andy is remembered by many for his ill-fortune with injuries. His worst was picked up following a head knock at Third Lanark's Cathkin Park in 1961. The injury sustained in a clash of heads with Third's right-back Jim Lewis developed into a near fatal case of meningitis. It is no exaggeration to say that he was critically ill – for several days he lay in a coma, and he was out of football until late 1961. The injury cast a huge cloud over Fir Park and drew the club together; indeed Ian St John, who was anxious to obtain a transfer, shelved his request for the meantime.

A distinctive feature of Andy's game was his ability to score direct from corners. A gentleman off the field, Andy rarely lost his temper on it, but Motherwell fans fondly recall one hilarious incident at Ibrox when, in a moment of rashness, Andy clashed with Bobby Shearer. A swift left hook from Andy was totally out of character, and Shearer, one of the hardest men in his day, promptly chased Andy up the wing. It is undoubtedly with a smile that Motherwell fans recall the career of Andy Weir: immensely skilful, extremely fast and very brave – a rare combination indeed.

Appearances 202 Goals 45

Hastie WEIR

A notable amateur with Queen's Park, Hastie won 4 caps at that level for Scotland. He stayed with the Spiders for four years before joining Motherwell on 3 August 1954, as a direct replacement for the veteran John Johnston.

His debut was a testing occasion, Motherwell struggling to a 4-4 draw with St Mirren. Within months the club had reached a League Cup final, and fallen 2-4 to Hearts. Relegation soon stalked the corridors of Fir Park and were it not for League reconstruction the club would have gone down. Although an agile 'keeper, he did have a few games that bordered on the disastrous, with seven-goal thumpings from both Hearts and Hibs in 1955/56 being amongst the worst.

Hastie Weir

At the age of thirty-one Hastie, who never played full-time, was asked by his employers to take up an engineering post in Ranchi, India. Understandably he did so, but returned to Scotland a few months later and was fixed up by Partick Thistle manager Willie Thornton for one season, before finally hanging up his boots and concentrating on his business career.

Appearances 193 Goals 0

Ian WEIR

At one stage there were three Weirs on the books at Motherwell and remarkably they played in the same team on several occasions. Ian's task was to take over the problematic left-back role, the departure of Archie Shaw creating a huge vacuum. He did so for most of the 1960/61 season, which was rather convenient as he lived just around the corner from the ground. Standing at 6 ft in his stocking soles, the Perth-born lad was a powerful player but unable to fend off the challenge presented by Matt Thomson when the latter arrived from Ardeer. Ian moved to Stirling Albion in 1962.

Appearances 22 Goals 0

Jim WEIR

Snapped up from KSV Hessen Kasselin in 1985, Jim lasted only one season at Fir Park before being freed in 1986. He

Ian Weir

cost the club £20,000 and had signed a two-year contract, but never fulfilled the expectations placed on his shoulders.

Appearances 2/1 Goals 0

Mickey WEIR
Weir was a diminutive winger who was recruited from Hibernian after a lengthy and devoted spell with the Hibees. There had been a short spell in England with Luton sandwiched between two periods at Hibernian, but in truth Mickey was a Hibee through and through.

He came to Motherwell in the veteran stages of his career but gave wonderful service and even scored against his beloved Hibs. His most famous goal came in the dramatic 2-2 draw with Dunfermline on the last day of the 1996/97 season. When his playing days ended he became a coach at Fir Park.
Appearances 23 Goals 6

Derek WELDON
Midfielder Derek signed for Motherwell as a twenty-one-year-old in February 1984 from Shotts Bon Accord. He made two appearances in March, against Hibernian and Celtic (SC) and it could be argued justifiably that he was thrown in at the deep end far too soon, to the great detriment of his career. Under Tommy McLean in 1984/85 he had a handful of reserve appearances before being released.
Appearances 1/1 Goals 0

Davie WHITEFORD
Whiteford was a right-back who joined the club in 1965 from Jordanhill Training College and was noted for his thrusting style and eye for goal. He came from good footballing stock.

Mickey Weir

Davie Whiteford

His father Jock, a centre half, had served Rutherglen Glencairn when they won the Junior Cup in 1939, and then turned senior with Ayr United, Stirling Albion and Hamilton Accies.

Davie's brother John was a Hibs stalwart and then an Airdrie star before being freed by Dumbarton late in the 1970s, and at that time cousin Derek Whiteford was still with Dumbarton, having previously served Airdrie.

Throughout his spell at Motherwell Davie was a part-timer, teaching physical education at a school in Wishaw. He enjoyed an impressive debut against Rangers at Ibrox in 1966 and in his seven years at Fir Park was reliable and adept from the penalty mark. Indeed, he was known for the power of his shooting. Davie left Motherwell for Falkirk in February 1974, and spent three seasons at Brockville and a further three with East Stirlingshire before he ended his football career with a season at Rutherglen Glencairn in Junior football.

Appearances 197 Goals 13

Archie WILLIAMS

Few players who play in a 6-6 draw and score a hat-trick are likely to be forgotten. Archie joined Motherwell just before they won the Scottish Cup in April 1952 and cost £1,000 from Hearts. In his first full season Motherwell were relegated and, although a clever left-winger, his slight frame put him at a disadvantage when facing robust defenders. Into the 'B' Division Motherwell went and they raced to the title, but managed to draw 6-6 against lowly Dumbarton – the highest scoring League draw ever in British football. Archie scored three that day, but even this could not guarantee him a place forever at Fir Park. In 1956 he left on

Archie Williams

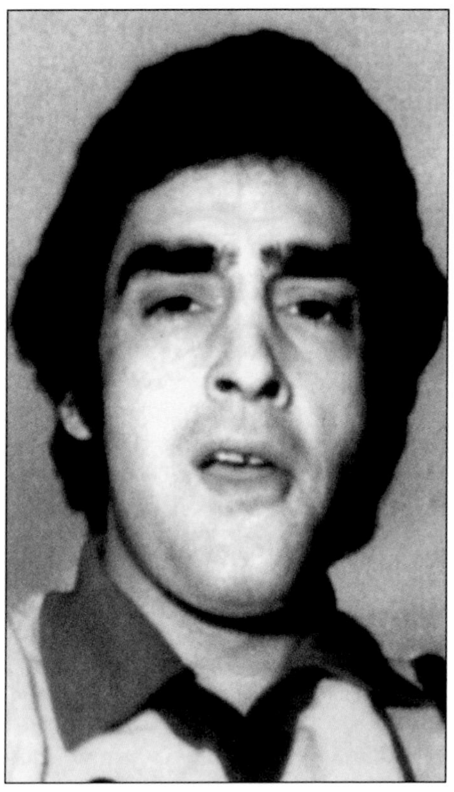

Paul Wilson

a free transfer but his four years at the club had included so much drama that it doubtless felt like much, much longer to Archie!

Appearances 36 Goals 11

Derek WILLIAMS
A young outside-left who stayed at Fir Park for two seasons only, Williams had a handful of reserve appearances. He was released in 1982, having played just one match.
Appearances 1 Goals 0

Lawrie WILLIAMS
More readily associated with Dumbarton, for whom he played many years, Lawrie had a brief spell with Motherwell during a goalkeeping crisis in 1980.
Appearances 4 Goals 0

Jimmy WILSON
Wilson came to Fir Park in a deal which took George Murray to Aberdeen in 1967. A dashing little winger, he had the added advantage of being able to take goals as well as make them. He moved to Dundee in 1970.
Appearances 84 Goals 12

Paul WILSON
Born in Milngavie, Glasgow, Paul joined Celtic in 1967 and eventually occupied the left-wing berth at Parkhead. He was capped by Scotland in 1975 and made over 100 League outings for the Celts before joining Motherwell in September 1978 for £50,000. He did not stay long at Fir Park, making only 21 League appearances and scoring once before he was moved on to Partick Thistle in July 1979. He eventually went into the junior ranks, played for Blantyre Celtic and was capped by Junior Scotland.
Appearances 18/3 Goals 1

Fraser WISHART
A full-back, Fraser joined Motherwell in 1983 from Pollok Juniors. By 1987 he was an ever present in the side and Motherwell's Player of the Year. Speedy on the overlap, solid in the tackle and an excellent reader of the game around him, he developed into a mainstay of Motherwell's side. Inevitably when a player shines so brightly, the scouts are attracted. St Mirren were at that time arguably the most ambitious side in Scotland and they spent £285,000 to take Fraser to Love Street.

Sadly, three years later Saints were

Fraser Wishart

relegated and faced a financial crisis – so much so that they went so far as to release Fraser on a free transfer! After an agonising six months out of football he joined Falkirk in November 1992, but the same fate – relegation – lay in store and again he was freed. At this stage luck finally shone on Fraser and Walter Smith stepped in to take him to Ibrox. Although a squad player, he acquitted himself superbly when called upon. Tommy McLean, who managed Hearts at the time, proved himself to be a supreme bargain hunter when he took Fraser to Hearts for just £50,000.

In the summer of 1996 Alex McLeish enticed him back to Fir Park. An eloquent and educated man who had represented his fellow professionals, he stayed for a season before moving on to Clydebank and then Airdrie, where he ended his senior career.

Appearances 169/8 Goals 5

Stevie WOODS

A bright young goalkeeper, Stevie started out with Hibernian but failed to play for their first team and made his breakthrough with Clydebank. From the Bankies, where he excelled, he moved to England with Preston North End and it was from Deepdale that Motherwell signed him for £75,000 in 1994. He had to compete with Scott Howie for first team openings, but did so with vigour and was the regular Motherwell goalkeeper until the arrival of Andy Goram. However, Goram was in the veteran stages during his time at Fir Park and thus Stevie had ample opportunities to stand in.

Appearances 63 Goals 0

Stevie Woods

Brian Wright

Brian WRIGHT

Brian's name is most readily linked with Clydebank, for whom he not only played twice but also coached. A tall and elegant midfielder, he was born in 1958 and initially joined Hamilton from Phoenix BC in 1975. He became a skilled midfielder and it cost Motherwell £18,000 to prise him away from Douglas Park in 1985. He made quite an impact at Fir Park and was a definite success.

He moved to Clydebank in 1987 and gave them excellent service. A brief spell with Partick Thistle saw him quickly rejoin the Bankies. In the mid-1990s he was first team coach at Clydebank, who did not employ a manager as such. Given that he made over 260 outings for Accies and a very high total for Bankies too, it is clear that Motherwell did not get the best out of him.

Appearances 67/7 Goals 6

Alan WYLLIE

A long-serving goalkeeper who never quite established himself as the regular number 1, Wyllie was signed from Penicuik Athletic. His early career was disrupted first by National Service, and then by the excellent form of Hastie Weir. He finally made his debut in a 2-5 home defeat by Falkirk in October 1957 and not until 1963/64 did he manage to make his mark (in that season he missed only three games). He remained a part-time player until the beginning of the 1960/61 campaign. He played his last game in the 1966/67 season and, despite a full ten years at the club, did not have many more than 100 appearances to his name.

Alan Wyllie

The highlight of his stay was probably starring in the winning side in the Second Eleven cup in 1954.

Once freed, he joined Cowdenbeath who were managed by the former Rangers and East Fife stalwart Andy Matthew. Tragically, Alan was killed in a car crash when he was only thirty-six years old.

Appearances 134 Goals 0

Bobby YOUNG

An exciting schoolboy talent, Bobby was spotted playing as a winger by the legendary Bobby Ancell and signed as such. Remarkably, he was actually a centre forward and had won 4 Scotland schoolboy caps in that position. Used sparingly in his early days, he rewarded Ancell with a series of cultured displays and played in the memorable floodlight friendlies against both Gothenburg and Flamengo. However, his stay at Fir Park was brief and within three years he had departed.

Bobby Young

Signed in 1959 from Neilston Victoria, Bobby's Motherwell claim to fame was a dramatic eighty-ninth minute equaliser against Celtic in January 1962, and a couple of weeks later he netted in a 3-1 win over Dundee, the eventual League champions. That win at Dens was marred by a tackle from Ian Ure, which left Bobby with ligament damage. It should be noted that instant and expert treatment was not available in those days and Bobby can still recall returning to Glasgow by train, and catching a bus back to Neilston – thus of course exacerbating the injury and arriving home in considerable pain.

The next stop for Bobby, who saw himself as a centre forward, was St Johnstone in 1962, and while there he hit over twenty goals as the Saints won a Second Division title. Jimmy McGrory, the Celtic boss, was impressed and snapped Bobby up, but a few frustrating months later Bobby moved to Dundee United. From Tannadice he journeyed in 1966 to Airdrie, then on to Berwick Rangers and finally Dumbarton.

Upon quitting the senior ranks, Bobby dropped to the junior scene where he made quite an impression. He spent six years with Saltcoats Victoria, which took him from player to coach then manager. Neilston was the next port of call and he guided the club to their first trophy in twenty years.

Appearances 26 Goals 6

'Tired but triumphant'... Fraser Wishart, Stevie Kirk and John Philliben celebrate a goal at Fir Park against Dundee United.

Appendix

MOTHERWELL MANAGERS

	IN	OUT
John Sailor Hunter	April 1911	May 1946
George Stevenson	April 1946	May 1955
Bobby Ancell	July 1955	June 1965
Bobby Howitt	March 1965	March 1973
Ian St John	June 1973	September 1974
Willie McLean	September 1974	December 1977
Roger Hynd	December 1977	November 1978
Ally MacLeod	December 1978	August 1981
Davie Hay	September 1981	May 1982
Jock Wallace	June 1982	November 1983
Bobby Watson	November 1983	May 1984
Tommy McLean	June 1984	July 1994
Alex McLeish	July 1994	February 1998
Harri Kampman	February 1998	October 1998
Billy Davies	October 1998	

APPENDIX

MOTHERWELL'S LEADING GOALSCORERS FROM 1946/47

1946/47	John Brown 16, Gordon Bremner 7
1947/48	Wilson Humphries 19
1948/49	Davie Mathie 13
1949/50	Archie Kelly 15, Jimmy Watson 9
1950/51	Jim Forrest 14, Archie Kelly 13
1951/52	Archie Kelly 20, Johnny Aitkenhead 10
1952/53	Archie Kelly 19
1953/54	Jackie Hunter 28, Jim Forrest 24
1954/55	Jackie Hunter 8, Charlie Aitken 8
1955/56	Ian Gardiner 9
1956/57	Ian Gardiner 18, Jackie Hunter 16
1957/58	Ian Gardiner 18, Ian St John 17
1958/59	Ian St John 24, Pat Quinn 13
1959/60	Ian St John 21, Pat Quinn 16
1960/61	Ian St John 18, Pat Quinn 18
1961/62	Pat Quinn 15, Pat Delaney 12
1962/63	Joe McBride 11
1963/64	Joe McBride 19
1964/65	Joe McBride 21

1965/66	Ian Thomson 10, Benny Cairney 7
1966/67	Bobby Campbell 18, 'Dixie' Deans 11
1967/68	'Dixie' Deans 11
1968/69	'Dixie' Deans 30, Tom Forsyth 13
1969/70	'Dixie' Deans 15
1970/71	'Dixie' Deans 9
1971/72	Jim MacCabe 7
1972/73	Billy McClymont 6, Kirkie Lawson 5
1973/74	Bobby Graham 13, John Goldthorp 10
1974/75	Willie Pettigrew 20, Bobby Graham 11
1975/76	Willie Pettigrew 22
1976/77	Wilie Pettigrew 21
1977/78	Vic Davidson 8, Willie Pettigrew 7
1978/79	Willie Pettigrew 6, Ian Clinging 5
1979/80	Willie Irvine 13, Brian McLaughlin 11
1980/81	Albert Kidd 13, Willie Irvine 12
1981/82	Willie Irvine 20, Brian McLaughlin 19
1982/83	Brian McClair 11
1983/84	John Gahagan 7
1984/85	Andy Harrow 9, Rab Stewart 9
1985/86	John Reilly 9

1986/87	Andy Walker 10, Stevie Kirk 10
1987/88	Steve Cowan 9, Ray Farningham 6
1988/89	Steve Kirk 14
1989/90	Nick Cusack 11
1990/91	Dougie Arnott 14
1991/92	Dougie Arnott 8, Steve Kirk 6
1992/93	Steve Kirk 10
1993/94	Tommy Coyne 12
1994/95	Tommy Coyne 16, Dougie Arnott 10
1995/96	Willie Falconer 5
1996/97	Tommy Coyne 11
1997/98	Tommy Coyne 15
1998/99	Owen Coyle 7, John Spencer 7
1999/2000	John Spencer 11, Lee McCulloch 9

MOST LEAGUE APPEARANCES SINCE 1946/47

(The following list shows those players to have played in each League fixture in a season)

1946/47	John Johnston, Willie Kilmarnock, Archie Shaw, Donald McLeod
1947/48	John Johnston, Wilson Humphries
1948/49	John Johnston
1949/50	None
1950/51	Willie Kilmarnock
1951/52	Willie Kilmarnock, Archie Kelly
1952/53	John Johnston
1953/54	John Johnston, Willie Kilmarnock, Willie Redpath
1954/55	Willie Kilmarnock
1955/56	Willie Kilmarnock, Hastie Weir
1956/57	Hastie Weir
1957/58	Charlie Aitken,
1958/59	Willie McSeveney, Andy Weir
1959/60	Pat Quinn, Willie Hunter
1960/61	None
1961/62	Pat Quinn
1962/63	George Lindsay
1963/64	None
1964/65	None
1965/66	Bobby McCallum, George Murray
1966/67	Willie McCallum, Bobby Campbell
1967/68	Peter McCloy, Davie Whiteford, John Martis
1968/69	Joe Wark, Tom Donnelly, Bobby McCallum
1969/70	Joe Wark, Tom Forsyth
1970/71	Davie Whiteford, Joe Wark
1971/72	None
1972/73	Davie Whiteford
1973/74	Joe Wark
1974/75	None
1975/76	Stuart Rennie, Joe Wark
1976/77	Gregor Stevens, Willie Pettigrew
1977/78	None
1978/79	None

1979/80	Hugh Sproat
1980/81	None
1981/82	Willie Irvine, John Gahagan
1982/83	None
1983/84	None
1984/85	None
1985/86	None
1986/87	Fraser Wishart, Paul Smith
1987/88	Craig Paterson
1988/89	Tom Boyd, Steve Kirk
1989/90	Ally Maxwell
1990/91	Ally Maxwell, Chris McCart
1991/92	None
1992/93	Brian Martin,
1993/94	Sieb Dykstra
1994/95	Paul Lambert
1995/96	Scott Howie
1996/97	None
1997/98	Owen Coyle
1998/99	None
1999/2000	None

Owen Coyle was a prolific marksman for Motherwell, and enjoyed the art of celebration.

MOTHERWELL'S LEAGUE RECORD

Season	P	W	D	L	F	A	Pts	Position
1946/47	30	12	5	13	58	54	29	8
1947/48	30	13	3	14	45	47	29	8
1948/49	30	10	5	15	44	49	25	12
1949/50	30	10	5	15	53	58	25	10
1950/51	30	11	6	13	58	65	28	9
1951/52	30	12	7	11	51	57	31	7
1952/53	30	10	5	15	57	80	25	15(R)
1953/54 (B)	30	21	3	6	109	43	45	1(P)
1954/55	30	9	4	17	42	62	22	17
1955/56	34	11	11	12	53	59	33	10
1956/57	34	16	5	13	72	66	37	7
1957/58	34	12	8	14	68	67	32	8
1958/59	34	18	8	8	83	50	44	3
1959/60	34	16	8	10	71	61	40	5
1960/61	34	15	8	11	70	57	38	5
1961/62	34	13	6	15	65	62	32	9
1962/63	34	10	11	13	60	63	31	10
1963/64	34	9	11	14	51	62	29	11
1964/65	34	10	8	16	45	54	28	14
1965/66	34	12	4	18	52	69	28	13
1966/67	34	10	11	13	59	60	31	10
1967/68	34	6	7	21	40	66	19	17(R)
1968/69 (2)	36	30	4	2	112	23	64	1 (P)
1969/70	34	11	10	13	49	51	32	11
1970/71	34	13	8	13	43	47	34	9
1971/72	34	11	7	16	49	69	29	10
1972/73	34	11	9	14	38	48	31	8
1973/74	34	14	7	13	45	40	35	9
1974/75	34	14	5	15	52	57	33	10
1975/76	34	16	8	12	57	49	40	4
1976/77	36	10	12	14	57	60	32	7
1977/78	36	13	7	16	45	52	33	6

Season	P	W	D	L	F	A	Pts	Position
1978/79	36	5	7	24	33	86	17	10 (R)
1979/80 (F)	39	16	11	12	59	48	43	6
1980/81 (F)	39	19	11	9	65	51	49	5
1981/82 (F)	39	26	9	4	92	36	61	1 (P)
1982/83	36	11	5	20	39	73	27	8
1983/84	36	4	7	25	31	75	15	10 (R)
1984/85 (F)	39	21	8	10	62	36	50	1 (P)
1985/86	36	7	6	23	33	36	20	9
1986/87	44	11	12	21	43	64	34	8
1987/88	44	13	10	21	37	56	36	8
1988/89	36	7	13	16	35	44	27	9
1989/90	36	11	12	13	43	47	34	6
1990/91	36	12	9	15	51	50	33	6
1991/92	44	10	14	20	43	61	34	10
1992/93	44	11	13	20	46	62	35	9
1993/94	44	20	14	10	58	43	54	3
1994/95	36	14	12	10	50	50	54	2
1995/96	36	9	12	15	28	39	39	8
1996/97	36	9	11	16	44	55	38	8
1997/98	36	9	7	20	46	64	34	9
1998/99	36	10	11	15	35	54	41	7
1999/00	36	14	10	12	49	63	52	4

KEY

(R) relegated
(P) promoted
(B) 'B' Division
(2) Second Division
(F) First Division

MOTHERWELL'S LEADING POST WAR APPEARANCES
(to the end of the 1999/2000 season)

League Appearances

Joe Wark	464 (5)
Willie Kilmarnock	452
John Johnston	323
Charlie Aitken	313
Archie Shaw	313
John Philliben	302
Andy Paton	301
Stevie Kirk	301
John Martis	297
Willie McCallum	277
Chris McCart	260
Tom Boyd	256
Bert McCann	246
Dougie Arnott	240
Brian Martin	237
Ian MacLeod	236 (7)
Willie Hunter	229
Willie Redpath	226
Jim Forrest	215
Andy Weir	202
Wilson Humphries	199
Davie Whiteford	197
Willie McSeveney	197
Pat Quinn	196
Jimmy Watson	195
Jamie Dolan	194
Hastie Weir	193
John Gahagan	191 (93)
Bobby Watson	179 (3)
Stuart Rennie	174
Matt Thomson	172
Johnny Aitkenhead	171
Graeme Forbes	169 (16)
Fraser Wishart	169 (8)
Peter Millar	165 (14)

George Lindsay	159
Pat Delaney	158
Willie Pettigrew	157 (9)
Davie Cooper	157
Bobby Campbell	157
Bobby McCallum	157
Craig Paterson	154 (4)
John 'Dixie' Deans	152
Tom Forsyth	150

MOTHERWELL'S LEADING POST WAR GOALSCORERS

(League goals to the end of the 1999/2000 season)

Pat Quinn	83
Willie Pettigrew	80
Ian St John	80
'Dixie' Deans	78
Wilson Humphries	69
Archie Kelly	66
Jimmy Watson	66
Stevie Kirk	63
Dougie Arnott	59
Tommy Coyne	59
Jim Forrest	58
Jackie Hunter	55
Joe McBride	51
Willie Irvine	49
Ian Gardiner	47
Andy Weir	45
John Goldthorp	43
Willie Hunter	40

MOTHERWELL'S INTERNATIONAL PLAYERS

Full International Appearances

Scotland (since the club's foundation)

Blair, J (1)	1934 *v.* W
Boyd, T (4)	1991 *v.* R, Sw, Bul, USSR
Cooper, D (2)	1990 *v.* N, Eg
Craig, A (3)	1929 *v.* N, Ho; 1932 *v.* E
Forrest , J(1)	1958 *v.* E
Humphries, W (1)	1952 *v.* Se
Hunter, W (3)	1960 *v.* H, T, 1961 *v.* W
Lambert, P (2)	1995 *v.* J, Ec
Macfadyen, W (2)	1934 *v.* A, W
Martin, B (2)	1995 *v.* J, Ec
Martis, J (1)	1961 *v.* W
McCann, R (5)	1959 *v.* WG; 1960 *v.* E, Ni, W, 1961 *v.* E
McClory, A (3)	1927 *v.* W, 1928 *v.* Ni, 1935 *v.* W
McKinnon, R (3)	1994 *v.* Ma; 1995 *v.* J, Fa
McMenemy, J (1)	1934 *v.* W
Murdoch, J (1)	1931 *v.* Ni
O'Donnell, P (1)	1994 *v.* Sw
Ogilvie, D (1)	1934 *v.* A
Paton, A (3)	1946 *v.* Bel, 1952 *v.* D, Se
Pettigrew, W (5)	1976 *v.* Sw, Ni, W; 1977 *v.* W, Se
Quinn, P (4)	1961 *v.* E, Ei(2); 1962 *v.* U
Redpath, W (9)	1949 *v.* W, Ni; 1951 *v.* E, D, F , Bel, A; 1952 *v.* Ni, E
Robertson, C (1)	1910 *v.* W
St John, I (7)	1959 *v.* WG; 1960 *v.* E, Ni, W, Pol, A; 1961 *v.* E
Stevenson, G (12)	1928 *v.* W, Ni; 1930 *v.* Ni, E, F; 1931 *v.* E, W; 1932 *v.* W, Ni, 1933 v Ni, 1934 *v.* E; 1935 *v.* Ni
Telfer, W (2)	1933 *v.* Ni, 1934 *v.* Ni
Wales, H, (1)	1933 *v.* W
Watson, J (1)	1948 *v.* Ni
Watson, R (1)	1971 *v.* USSR
Weir, A (6)	1959 *v.* WG, 1960 *v.* E, P, A, H, T

Wales

Ellis, B (6)	1932 *v.* E; 1933 *v.* E, S; 1934 *v.* S; 1936 *v.* E; 1937 *v.* S

Ireland

Murray, J (2)	1910 *v.* E, S

Northern Ireland

O'Neill, C (3)	1989 *v.* Ch; 1990 *v.* Ei; 1991 *v.* D

Republic of Ireland

Coyne, T (13)	1994 *v.* Ru, Ho, Bel, G, CzR, I , M , Ho; 1995 *v.* Lie, Ni, A; 1996 *v.* Ru; 1998 *v.* Bel

Finland

Valakari, S

Under 23 Appearances – Scotland

Delaney, P (3), Forsyth, T (1), Hunter, W (4), MacRae, K (2), Martis, J (1), McVie, W (2);
Murray, G (3); Pettigrew, W (7); Roberts, R (1); St John, I (3); Weir, A (3)

Under 21 Appearances – Scotland

Boyd, T (5); Lindsay, J (1); McCulloch, L (14); McGrillen, P (2); McMillan, S (4); O'Donnell, P (8); Stevens, G (1)

Scottish League Appearances

Aitken, C (2); Aitkenhead, J (3); Blair, J (2); Boyd, T (1); Bremner, H (1); Brown, C (1); Craig, A(1); Ellis, B (1); Ferguson, H (3); Ferrier, R (7); Forsyth, T (1); Hampton, C. M. (1); Humphries, W (1); Hunter, W (4); Jackson, J (1); Kilmarnock, W (1); Macfadyen, W (1); MacRae, K (1); McBride, J (2); McCallum, R (1); McCann, R (5); McClory, A (2); McKenzie, T (2); McCloy, P (2); McMenemy, J (3); Millar, P (1); Murray, G (1); Pettigrew, W (2); Quinn, P (6); Rankin, W. (3); Redpath, W. (5); Roberts, R (1); Shaw, A (2); St John, I (4); Stevens, G (1); Stevenson, G. (10); Stewart, A (1); Telfer, W. (1); Thackeray, D. (1); Wark, J (1); Watson, J (1); Weir, A (1)

B Internationals

Aitken, C (1)	1957 *v.* England
Gardiner, I (1)	1957 *v.* England
Boyd, T (5)	1986 *v.* West Germany, Ire; 1987 *v.* Ire, Belgium, 1990 *v.* Yugoslavia

Wartime Internationals

Kilmarnock, W (1)	*v.* England 1944
Paton, A (2)	*v.* Wales 1945, Ireland 1945
Bremner, G (1)	*v.* England 1943

MOTHERWELL PLAYERS WITH MORE THAN FOUR GOALS IN A GAME

George Watson (6)	away *v.* Falkirk, 27 October 1928 (League)
Alex Stewart (6)	home *v.* Celtic, 30 April, 1937 (League)
Wilson Humphries (6)	home *v.* Dundee United , 23 January 1954 (League)

(Willie Macfadyen *v.* South Africa and Ian St John *v.* Flamengo each scored a double hat-trick in a friendly)

Hugh Ferguson (5)	home *v.* Clydebank, 10 December 1921 (League)
Hugh Ferguson (5)	home *v.* Galston, 24 January 1925 (Scottish Cup)

Willie Macfadyen (5)	home *v.* Third Lanark, 16 September 1931 (League)
Willie Macfadyen (5)	home *v.* Third Lanark, 3 December 1932 (League)
Willie Macfadyen (5)	home *v.* Montrose, 4 February 1933 (Scottish Cup)
Willie Macfadyen (5)	away *v.* Queen of the South, 26 August 1933 (League)
Robert Russell (5)	home *v.* Falkirk, 11 August 1962 (League Cup)
Bobby Campbell (5)	away *v.* St. Mirren, 24 September 1966 (League)
Vic Davidson (5)	home *v.* Alloa Athletic, 6 August 1977 (Anglo-Scottish Cup)

(John Quinn and Willie Macfadyen both scored five goals in friendly fixtures)

MOTHERWELL'S SCOTTISH CUP TRIUMPHS

1951/52

First Round (January 26)
Forfar Athletic 2, Motherwell 4 (Kelly, Watson, Sloan and o.g.)
Motherwell: Johnston, Kilmarnock, Shaw; McLeod, Paton, Redpath, Sloan, Humphries, Kelly, Watson, Aitkenhead.

Second Round (February 9)
St. Mirren 2, Motherwell 3 (Humphries, Watson, Sloan)
Motherwell: Johnston, Kilmarnock, Shaw; Cox, Paton, Redpath, Sloan, Humphries, Kelly, Watson, Aitkenhead.

Third Round (February 23)
Dunfermline Athletic 1, Motherwell 1 (Watson)
Motherwell: Johnston, Kilmarnock, Shaw; Cox, Paton, Redpath, Sloan, Humphries, Kelly, Watson, Aitkenhead.
Third Round replay (February 27)
Motherwell 4, Dunfermline Athletic 0 (Kelly, Aitkenhead 2, Humphries)
Motherwell: Johnston, Kilmarnock, Shaw; Cox, Paton, Redpath, Sloan, Humphries, Kelly, Watson, Aitkenhead.

Quarter Final (March 8)
Rangers 1, Motherwell 1 (Sloan)
Motherwell: Johnston, Kilmarnock, Shaw; Cox, Paton, Redpath, Sloan, Humphries, Kelly, Watson, Aitkenhead.
Quarter Final replay (March 12)

Motherwell 2, Rangers 1 (Aitkenhead, Humphries)
Motherwell: Johnston, Kilmarnock, Shaw; Cox, Paton, Redpath, Sloan, Humphries, Kelly, Watson, Aitkenhead.

Semi Final (March 29)
Heart of Midlothian 1, Motherwell 1 (Watson)
Motherwell: Johnston, Kilmarnock, Shaw; Cox, Paton, Redpath, Sloan, Humphries, Kelly, Watson, Aitkenhead.
Semi Final Replay (April 7)
Heart of Midlothian 1, Motherwell 1 (Watson)
Motherwell: Johnston, Kilmarnock, Shaw; Cox, Paton, Redpath, Sloan, Humphries, Kelly, Watson, Aitkenhead.
Semi Final Second Replay (April 9)
Heart of Midlothian 1, Motherwell 3 (Shaw, Humphries, Redpath)
Motherwell: Johnston, Kilmarnock, Shaw; Cox, Paton, Redpath, Sloan, Humphries, Kelly, Watson, Aitkenhead.

Final (April 19)
Dundee 0, Motherwell 4 (Watson, Redpath, Humphries, Kelly)
Motherwell: Johnston, Kilmarnock, Shaw; Cox, Paton, Redpath, Sloan, Humphries, Kelly, Watson, Aitkenhead.

1952 Facts and Figures: Motherwell played ten games to win the Scottish Cup. In nine of those games they fielded exactly the same starting line-up, the exception being the first match in which McLeod played in place of Cox. In the game at St Mirren, Motherwell trailed 2-0 at half-time. All three semi final ties, and the final itself, were played at Hampden Park.

1990/91

Third Round (January 26)
Aberdeen 0, Motherwell 1 (Kirk)
Motherwell: Maxwell, Philliben, Boyd; O'Neill, Paterson, McCart; Arnott, Dolan, Ferguson, Angus, Cooper. Sub: Kirk

Fourth Round (February 23)
Motherwell 4, Falkirk 2 (McLeod, Cusack 2, Kirk)
Motherwell: Maxwell, Philliben, Boyd, O'Donnell, Paterson, McCart; McLeod, Ferguson, Cusack, Angus, Cooper. Sub: Kirk

Quarter Final (March 16)
Motherwell 0, Morton 0
Motherwell: Maxwell, Nijholt, Boyd, O'Donnell, Paterson, McCart; McLeod, Griffin, Arnott, Angus, Cooper.

Quarter Final Replay (March 19)
Morton 1, Motherwell 1 (Boyd)
Motherwell: Maxwell, Nijholt, Boyd; O'Neill, Paterson, McCart; Arnott, Russell, Cusack, Kirk, Cooper.
Won on penalties

Semi Final (April 3)
Celtic 0, Motherwell 0
Motherwell: Maxwell, Nijholt, Boyd; O'Neill, Philliben, McCart; Arnott, Griffin, Ferguson, O'Donnell, Angus
Semi Final Replay (April 9)
Celtic 2, Motherwell 4 (Arnott 2, O'Neill, Kirk)
Motherwell: Maxwell, Nijholt, Boyd; O'Neill, Philliben, McCart; Arnott, Griffin, Ferguson, O'Donnell, Angus

Final (May 18)
Dundee United 3, Motherwell 4 (Ferguson, O'Donnell, Angus, Kirk)
Motherwell: Maxwell, Nijholt, Boyd; Griffin, Paterson, McCart; Arnott, Angus, Ferguson, O'Donnell and Cooper
Subs: Kirk and O'Neill

Facts and Figures

Stevie Kirk came into the matches against Aberdeen, Falkirk Celtic and Dundee United as a substitute … and scored in each game! His goal against Aberdeen was with his first kick of the ball. One of Motherwell's favourite ex-players – Johnny Gahagan – scored the Morton goal in the 1-1 draw at Cappielow; Motherwell won the penalty shoot-out and Colin O'Neill celebrated with a 'Hugo Sanchez' style back-flip. Ally Maxwell spent two days in hospital after the final, having sustained serious internal injuries in the course of the game; he never played for the club again (neither did Tom Boyd, who moved to Chelsea in the summer). Phil O'Donnell's goal in the final was his first for the club.